NORTH DAKOTA WILDLIFE VIEWING GUIDE

Joseph Knue

FALCON PRESS

ACKNOWLEDGMENTS

Producing this book was a cooperative effort involving Defenders of Wildlife, the North Dakota Game and Fish Department, the North Dakota Parks and Tourism Department, the North Dakota Forest Service, the USDA Forest Service, the U.S. Fish and Wildlife Service, the National Park Service, the Bureau of Land Management, The Nature Conservancy, and Falcon Press.

The steering committee, which directed the development of the guide, included Ted Upgren and Randy Kreil, North Dakota Game and Fish Department; Donna Schouweiler and Bonnie Heidel, North Dakota Parks; Tracy Potter, North Dakota Tourism; Glenda Fauske, North Dakota Forest Service; Gary Foli, USDA Forest Service; Ken Torkelson, U.S. Fish and Wildlife Service; Terry Rich and Chris Kelsey, Bureau of Land Management; Bruce Kaye, National Park Service; and Lynn Alexander, The Nature Conservancy. The project coordinator from Defenders of Wildlife was Kate Davies; the project consultant from the USDA Forest Service was Jim Cole. The editor at Falcon Press was John Grassy.

Many others contributed to this project with site nominations, reviews of site descriptions, and tracking down countless details. Still others, too numerous to list, kindly offered their knowledge of wildlife and the relationships between wildlife and habitat.

Four people should be singled out for their extraordinary effort. The contributions of Ted Upgren, Jim Cole, Randy Kreil, and Bonnie Heidel can be seen on every page of this guide.

Front cover photo:

American bison, Theodore Roosevelt National Park. LYNN BENDER

Back cover photos:

Pintail drake, Long Lake National Wildlife Refuge. LYNN BENDER
J. Clark Salyer National Wildlife Refuge. KEITH KRAMER

CONTENTS

REGION THREE: WEST

Uncrowded compared to most national parks, the North Unit of Theodore Roosevelt National Park is among North Dakota's best sites for watching wildlife. There is tremendous diversity in this striking landscape. DAPHNE KINZLER

REGION FOUR: LAKES & GARDENS

State of North Dakota
OFFICE OF THE GOVERNOR
600 E. BOULEVARD · GROUND FLOOR
BISMARCK, NORTH DAKOTA 58505-0001
(701) 224-2200

Dear Reader,

North Dakota, John Steinbeck said, is where the map should fold, the true dividing line between east and west in America. He was right—and that meeting of two ecosystems at the Missouri River is what gives North Dakota the great diversity of wildlife we enjoy.

The rugged badlands of the west are home to large buffalo herds, mule deer, bighorn sheep, and a plethora of pheasants. Golden eagles and peregrine falcons ride the azure drafts overhead, prairie dogs dig tunnels underfoot, and sharptail grouse explode from the buffaloberries. East of the Missouri River lies the bountiful central flyway. It is the most productive waterfowl area in North America with countless potholes, sloughs, and crop "leftovers" to provide habitat and nourishment for waterfowl and wildlife of every sort. Here, white pelicans and piping plovers nest, and snow geese drop by to visit.

To the east and north are the forested areas of the Red and Sheyenne river valleys, the Pembina Gorge, and the Turtle Mountains. Moose and elk move through trees filled with songbirds. White-tailed deer drink from streams where muskrat and beaver have lived for centuries.

Warm people and wondrous seasons invite you to visit North Dakota. Use this book to *Discover the Spirit* of the state we're proud to call home.

Sincerely,

George A. Sinner

George A. Sinner
Governor

PROJECT SPONSORS

The mission of the BUREAU OF RECLAMATION is to manage, develop, and protect water and related land resources in an environmentally sound manner in the interest of the American people. The success of Reclamation programs can be seen in the benefits provided to not only the regional but also the national economy that will continue to be realized into the future. Reliable sources of water and energy are critical factors in sustaining long-term economic growth, improving the environment, and enhancing quality of life of all Americans. Continuing to meet the growing water demands and resource management needs of the West will be much more complex and

difficult in the future. Meeting these challenges requires innovations in water management, use, and development practices and technologies.

The mission of the NORTH DAKOTA GAME AND FISH DEPARTMENT is to protect, conserve, and enhance fish and wildlife populations and their habitats for sustained public consumptive and nonconsumptive use. North Dakota Game and Fish Department, 100 North Bismarck Expressway, Bismarck, North Dakota 58501-5095, (701) 221-6300.

The NORTH DAKOTA PARKS AND TOURISM DEPARTMENT plans and coordinates government programs encouraging the full development and preservation of existing and future parks, outdoor recreation areas, nature preserves, and promotes tourism to create new wealth for North Dakotans by utilizing a targeted marketing effort to attract out-of-state and in-state visitors. North Dakota Parks and Tourism Department, 604 East Boulevard Avenue, Bismarck, North Dakota 58505, (701) 224-2525.

The mission of THE NATURE CONSERVANCY is to preserve plants, animals, and natural communities that represent the diversity of life on Earth by protecting the lands and water they need to survive. The Nature Conservancy, Dakotas Field Office, 1014 East Central Avenue, Bismarck, North Dakota 58501.

The U.S. FISH AND WILDLIFE SERVICE is pleased to support the Watchable Wildlife effort in furtherance of its mission to preserve, protect, and enhance fish and wildlife resources and their habitats for the use and enjoyment of the American public. U.S. Fish and Wildlife Service, 1500 Capitol Avenue, Bismarck, North Dakota 58501.

The U.S. FOREST SERVICE, DEPARTMENT OF AGRICULTURE, has a mandate to protect, improve, and wisely use the nation's forest and range resources for multiple purposes to benefit all Americans. U.S. Forest Service, 1824 North 11th Street, Bismarck, North Dakota 58501.

The BUREAU OF LAND MANAGEMENT is responsible for the balanced management of the public lands and resources and their various values so that they are considered in a combination that will best serve the needs of the American people. Management is based upon the principles of multiple use and sustained yield, in a combination of uses that takes into account the long-term needs of future generations for renewable and nonrenewable resources. Bureau of Land Management, 2933 Third Avenue West, Dickinson, North Dakota, 58601.

DEFENDERS OF WILDLIFE is a national, nonprofit organization of more than 80,000 members and supporters dedicated to preserving the natural abundance and diversity of wildlife and its habitat. A one-year membership is $20 and includes six issues of the bimonthly magazine, *Defenders*. To join or for further information, write or call Defenders of Wildlife, 1244 Nineteenth Street, N.W., Washington, DC 20036, (202) 659-9510.

THE NATIONAL FISH AND WILDLIFE FOUNDATION, chartered by Congress to stimulate private giving to conservation, is an independent not-for-profit organization. Using federally funded challenge grants, it forges partnerships between the public and private sectors to conserve the nation's fish, wildlife, and plants. National Fish and Wildlife Foundation, 18th and C Street N.W., Washington, DC 20240, (202) 208-4051.

Other Important Contributors Include:

North Dakota Nongame Wildlife Program   North Dakota Project WILD
Theodore Roosevelt Nature and History Association   North Dakota Forest Service

INTRODUCTION

Just a little more than one hundred years after settlement, North Dakota remains a place for wildlife. It is, in fact, many places. The birds and animals you can watch here depends on where—and when—you go looking.

North Dakota is a place for waterfowl. In spring, its potholes and wetlands are the nation's duck factories. Come fall, they are stopovers for snow geese and tundra swans on their long high journey ahead of winter.

North Dakota is rivers—the Red River of the North, the Souris, the Little Missouri, the Yellowstone, and the Missouri itself, floated by the likes of Lewis and Clark, who along its banks saw elk, bison, and strange, swift animals that resembled goats or gazelles. Today we call them pronghorns.

North Dakota is badlands. The eerie, eroded landscape lives in the memory long after you leave, with images of bighorns clinging to steep slopes, of coyotes, mule deer, and golden eagles.

North Dakota is grassland—mixed-grass prairie, breeding grounds of the western meadowlark. Here, at sunrise on spring mornings, male sharp-tailed grouse gather to perform a courtship dance. In woody cover, white-tailed deer browse on emerging shoots. Ferruginous hawks—the "prairie eagle"—nest

Wild horses are historically important in the badlands, appearing in the writings of Theodore Roosevelt and others. The ecological significance of the animals is less well-understood, and is being studied. PAUL CHRISTIANSON

where there is native prairie. There are many other birds—upland plover, Sprague's pipit, brown-headed cowbird, chestnut-collared longspur, and a wide array of sparrows.

North Dakota is much more. The Pembina Hills, where aspen forest harbors moose, elk, and ruffed grouse. The Turtle Mountains, with deer, moose, ruffed grouse, and the snowshoe hare. The sandplains of the Sheyenne Grassland, North Dakota's only stronghold for the greater prairie chicken.

This is your guide to the places and wildlife that are North Dakota. You will find settings that seem untouched since the retreat of the ice age, and others that have been greatly altered by people. There are settings where people have worked to restore the land for wildlife. Each place has something to tell us. All of them offer something to enjoy.

THE WATCHABLE WILDLIFE PROGRAM

North Dakotans have been watching the state's wildlife for a long time now—long before Watchable Wildlife had a name. Consider Sullys Hill National Game Preserve, one of the wildlife viewing sites in this guide: North Dakotans were going there to watch wildlife when Theodore Roosevelt proclaimed it a national park in 1904. Or think of the late Wilson P. Sly of Enderlin, North Dakota: Mr. Sly personally put up and maintained over eighty bluebird boxes in the southeast corner of the state just because he liked to see bluebirds. More recently, when the North Dakota Game and Fish Department put an observation blind on a sharp-tailed grouse dancing ground in the spring of 1985, they had to start taking reservations to use it. And it's been booked every year since.

Examples like these can be found around the country. In retrospect, it seems surprising that it's taken so long for wildlife watching to get the kind of attention that hunting and fishing have had. But there's plenty of attention now, so much so that in 1990, eight federal agencies, four national conservation organizations, and the International Association of Fish and Wildlife Agencies signed a memorandum of understanding to develop a program around Watchable Wildlife.

The national Watchable Wildlife Program—of which this guide is a part—has particularly wide goals. These include efforts to accommodate the public interest in wildlife watching with a wide range of viewing opportunities, and assistance in finding those opportunities. That's what this guide series is all about. The guides, however, are only a step along the way. Interpretation and enhancement of viewing sites will help transform interest in watching wildlife into a broader sense of public responsibility for wildlife conservation.

Ultimately, the goal of the Watchable Wildlife Program is to create a new understanding and appreciation for the natural world in all its diversity. Each species—hunted or not, photographed or not—plays a part in the health of other species and of entire ecosystems. True conservation, and true appreciation, recognize and work to preserve such interdependence. The Watchable Wildlife Program is only a beginning.

VIEWING HINTS

The first and last hours of daylight are generally the best times to watch and photograph most wildlife. Spring and early summer are the best seasons for watching songbirds, nesting birds, and small mammals. Spring through summer is best for wildflowers. Fall is best for the annual migration of geese across North Dakota, and it is the only time that imitating a moose call might bring an animal into view.

Be quiet. Quick movements and loud noises generally scare wildlife. Learn to use vegetation, or your car or boat, as an observation blind. Very often you might see more by staying in your car. Learn to stay still for fairly long periods of time, and if you talk, keep your voice to a whisper. Avoid bright-colored clothing. Use as many viewing aids as possible. Binoculars or a spotting scope are standard equipment for a wildlife watcher. Field guides help with identification and can provide valuable information about habits and habitat. Be patient. Wait quietly for animals to enter or return to an area. Wait for animals to move within your view. More often than not, patience will reward you.

OUTDOOR ETHICS

•Honor the rights of private landowners. Gain permission before entering their property.

•Honor wildlife's need for free movement. Feeding, touching, or otherwise harassing wildlife is inappropriate. Young wild animals that appear to be alone have not been abandoned. Allow them to find their own way.

•Honor the rights of others to enjoy the experience of watching wildlife. Loud noises, quick movements, or any other behavior that might scare wildlife is inappropriate. Wait your turn or seek another viewing opportunity.

•Honor your own right to enjoy the outdoors in the future. Leave wildlife habitat in better condition than you found it. Pick up litter that you find at a viewing site and dispose of it properly.

HOW TO USE THIS GUIDE

This guide is organized around North Dakota's four travel regions. Each travel region forms a separate section of the book. The color strips on the pages are keyed to the travel regions for easy reference. Each section begins with a detailed map of the travel region, with viewing sites marked and numbered.

Wildlife **icons** indicate the animals you are most likely to see. Site **descriptions** describe the habitat and then identify some of the species to look for. Only unique or representative species are listed, not everything you might encounter.

Viewing information rounds out the picture, with notes on the best seasons for viewing, particular opportunities to take advantage of, and, occasionally, precautions. These include road conditions, safety, viewing limitations, and land ownership limitations.

Directions are based on the North Dakota Official Highway Map. Local roads—usually county roads—are described from maps prepared by North

Dakota's Department of Transportation. For sites where the written directions did not seem sufficient, a site map has been included.

Ownership indicates the agency or entity that owns or manages the site. The abbreviations are explained below. Private sites have been listed with the permission of the owner—please respect their rights and instructions when visiting these sites. Telephone numbers are listed in the event you need more information about individual sites. North Dakota has one **area code 701** for the entire state.

Each site description is followed by the name of the **closest town** to the site, along with facility and recreation icons. These icons are explained below.

SITE OWNERSHIP ABBREVIATIONS

USFWS	United States Fish and Wildlife Service
USFS	United States (Department of Agriculture) Forest Service
NPS	National Park Service
NDGF	North Dakota Game and Fish Department
NDPT	North Dakota Parks and Tourism Department
NDFS	North Dakota Forest Service
SHSND	State Historical Society of North Dakota
UND	University of North Dakota
BLM	Bureau of Land Management
BOR	Bureau of Reclamation
COE	Corps of Engineers
PVT	Private Ownership

FEATURED WILDLIFE

 Songbirds
 Upland Birds
 Waterfowl
 Wading Birds
 Shorebirds
 Birds of Prey
 Small Mammals

 Hoofed Mammals
 Carnivores Mammals
 Freshwater
 Fish Amphibians
 Reptiles,
Insects
Wildflowers

FACILITIES AND RECREATION

P Parking

Restrooms

Restaurant

Lodging

$ Fee

Picnic

Trails

Camping

Bicycling

Small Boats

Boat Ramp

Large Boats

Cross-country Skiing

Handicap Accessible

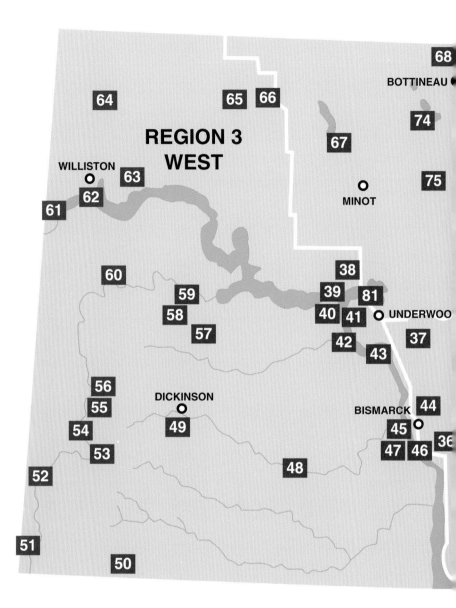

MAP INFORMATION

North Dakota is divided into four travel regions shown on this map. Wildlife viewing sites in this guide are numbered consecutively in a general pattern. Each region forms a seperate section in this book, and each section begins with a map of that region.

1 This symbol indicates the location and number of a wildlife viewing site.

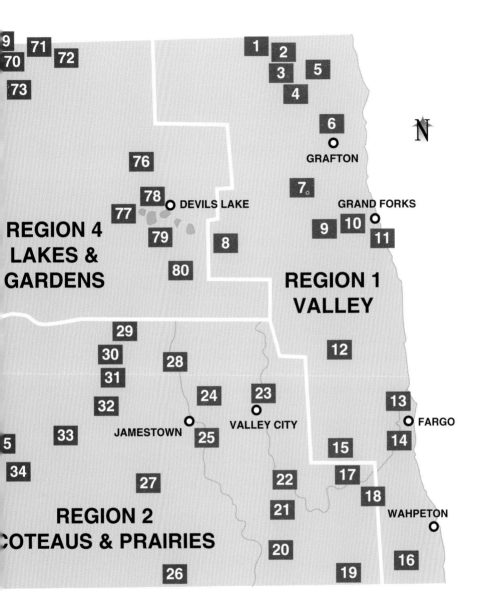

As you travel across North Dakota, look for these special highway signs that identify wildlife viewing sites. The binoculars logo and directional arrow will help guide you to the viewing area.

NOTE: It is very important to read the directions provided in each site description–highway signs may refer to more than one site along a particular route.

WHERE YOU ARE

North Dakota is more than one place. There are many ways to describe its variety. One of the ways is to divide the state into provinces—the semiarid Great Plains in the west, and the more humid Central Lowlands in the east. Another way is to talk about the ice age. Parts of North Dakota were greatly changed by ice age glaciers, and part was left alone. Even the glaciated parts of North Dakota vary greatly. There are flat lake plains, rolling plains mantled in soil and rock deposited by the moving glacier, and many other gouges, ridges, and hills associated with the advance, retreat, and melting of the ice sheet. In the unglaciated part of North Dakota, thousands of years of flowing water and wind have carved the surface.

North Dakota's variety was shaped by climate, elevation, soils, moisture, and wind. Its plants and animals have adapted to these conditions. They have adapted to each other as well, forming a community around special conditions of life, depending on these conditions and on each other. It's easy to see how, if the same conditions of life persist year after year, and the same plants and animals are there year after year, the communities of life become very stable. It's also easy to see that the more conditions of life there are, and the more different kinds of animals and plants there are, the more stable the community will be. It's a sort of disaster protection. The more diverse a community is, the more legs it has to stand on.

The idea that a diverse biological community is a strong community has great implications for North Dakota. Scattered through this guide are some examples of how biological communities work here, and some of the implications of change. There is almost always evidence of man-made change. It's something to think about as you visit the sites listed in this guide.

The hilly, deeply eroded surface of North Dakota's badlands creates large variations in slope, moisture, and temperature within very small areas. These variations give the badlands tremendous habitat diversity for wildlife. See page 68. KEITH KRAMER

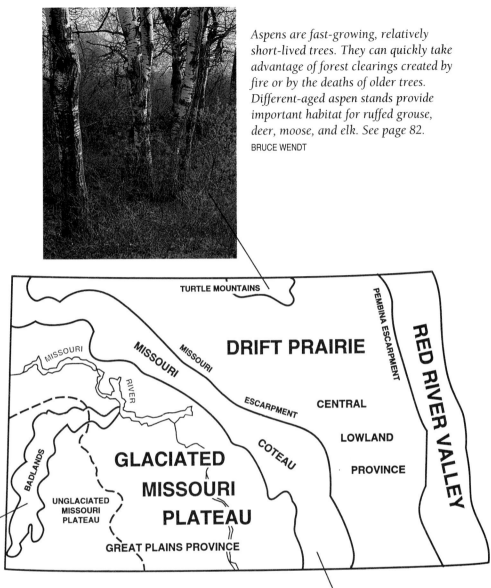

Aspens are fast-growing, relatively short-lived trees. They can quickly take advantage of forest clearings created by fire or by the deaths of older trees. Different-aged aspen stands provide important habitat for ruffed grouse, deer, moose, and elk. See page 82.
BRUCE WENDT

TURTLE MOUNTAINS

PEMBINA ESCARPMENT

DRIFT PRAIRIE

RED RIVER VALLEY

MISSOURI

MISSOURI

MISSOURI

RIVER

ESCARPMENT

CENTRAL

LOWLAND

PROVINCE

COTEAU

BADLANDS

GLACIATED MISSOURI PLATEAU

UNGLACIATED MISSOURI PLATEAU

GREAT PLAINS PROVINCE

Roughly two-thirds of North Dakota— the area north and east of the Missouri River—lies in North America's prairie pothole region. See page 42.
WILLIAM K. VINJE

15

REGION ONE: VALLEY

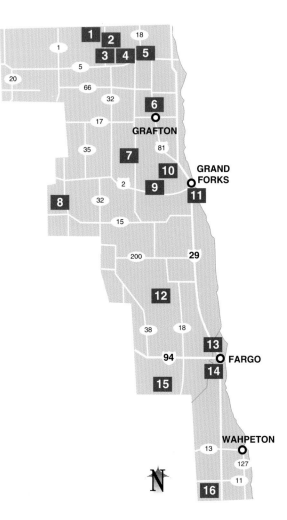

SITE 1	PEMBINA HILLS
SITE 2	TETRAULT WOODS STATE FOREST
SITE 3	JAY V. WESSELS WILDLIFE MANAGEMENT AREA
SITE 4	ICELANDIC STATE PARK
SITE 5	CAVALIER WOODS
SITE 6	ELMWOOD
SITE 7	FOREST RIVER BIOLOGY AREA
SITE 8	STUMP LAKE
SITE 9	TURTLE RIVER STATE PARK

SITE 10	KELLY'S SLOUGH NATIONAL WILDLIFE REFUGE
SITE 11	LINCOLN PARK AND RIVERSIDE PARK
SITE 12	ERIE DAM WILDLIFE MANAGEMENT AREA
SITE 13	OAK GROVE PARK
SITE 14	LINDENWOOD PARK
SITE 15	HAMILTON WILLS WILDLIFE MANAGEMENT AREA
SITE 16	MUEHLER PRAIRIE

Description: A deep, forested river valley, with some of the state's highest habitat diversity and its largest unbroken forest. In the Pembina Hills, forest is interspersed with shrub land, prairie, and wetlands. The area contains North Dakota's largest population of moose and its only naturally occurring herd of elk. It is good habitat for ruffed grouse and wild turkeys. More than seventy-five species of breeding birds are found here, including eleven of the state's fourteen breeding warblers. More than 480 species of plants have been identified, including thirty species rare to the state.

Viewing Information: The scenic Pembina Hills offer viewing opportunities by car, on foot, by cross-country skis, or by canoe. There are gravel roads throughout the area, but the roads are unmarked and can be treacherous when wet. Hiking and cross-country skiing are good in publicly owned areas. Driving in the area and finding public land are easier with county and topographic maps. The Pembina River can be floated by canoe in the spring and early summer.

Directions: From Walhalla, go five miles west on Cavalier County Road 55. Turn north and go for one mile; turn west, and follow the winding road to Wildlife Management Areas on the Pembina River and Little North Pembina River.

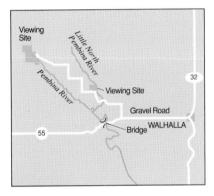

Ownership: NDGF (662-3617)
Size: 3,819 acres
Closest Town: Walhalla

Two hundred years ago, the Pembina Hills provided traders with furs, meat, and hides. The Hills are still rich in wildlife, harboring moose, elk, beaver, many species of birds, and perhaps the state's highest plant diversity.
CRAIG BIHRLE

17

2 TETRAULT WOODS STATE FOREST

Description: A small area with a mixture of forest, riverine wetland, brush, and grassland habitats. Following the Pembina River, the area provides a home to beaver and songbirds. Waterfowl and the occasional deer and heron can be seen in the fall.

Viewing Information: Best viewing is in the fall, when waterfowl, deer, and even an occasional moose or elk might be spotted. Beaver, songbirds, and raptors can be seen, especially in late summer and fall. A trail follows the windings of the Pembina River through the area. Take your binoculars. The trails are often wet and can be muddy underfoot.

Directions: From Walhalla, follow North Dakota 32 south 1.5 miles to the large sign on the west side of the highway. In wet weather and in winter it is best to park at this entrance and walk down the steep incline to the woods and the river. When leaving the area, use caution reentering North Dakota 32.

Ownership: NDFS (549-2441)
Size: 432 acres   **Closest Town:** Walhalla

North Dakota is home to three species of cottontails. These small mammals are an important source of food for foxes, eagles, coyotes, hawks, and owls. HAROLD UMBER

3 | JAY V. WESSELS WILDLIFE MANAGEMENT AREA

Description: An area of oak-aspen woodland with rolling, high water table sand hills and two wetland bogs. The area provides one of the best opportunities in the state for viewing moose . Other species to watch for are wild turkeys, ruffed grouse, and snowshoe hares. During spring migration, the site is good for woodland warblers.

Viewing Information: This site presents some interesting opportunities. In the fall (before hunting season), moose calling is a popular way to bring moose into view. Calling is also effective with coyotes, which frequent the area. Wild turkeys may be seen all year; ruffed grouse can be heard drumming in the spring. The peak season for warblers is mid-May to early June. Viewing from a vehicle is possible from the road that crosses the area east to west, and there are any number of undeveloped trails. Cross-country skiing is permitted (the trails are not groomed), as is horseback riding. Groups of twenty-five or more riders need a permit from the Game and Fish Department.

Directions: From Walhalla, take North Dakota 32 south for approximately seven miles, then turn east on the gravel road. Take this road 2.5 miles to the perimeter of the WMA.

Ownership: NDGF (662-3617)
Size: 3,343 acres   **Closest Town:** Walhalla

Moose are colonizers. Though their habitat is concentrated in areas such as the Pembina Hills, they have been spotted hundreds of miles away in North Dakota's semiarid southwest. TOM GIBSON

19

4 ICELANDIC STATE PARK

Description: The primary viewing area is in the Gunlogson Nature Preserve, a .75-mile wooded segment of the Tongue River. The forest is dominated by mature elm and basswood. Shallow ponds and wet thickets can be found in low-lying areas. In addition to the more common riverine forest plants and animals, more than a dozen rare species can be found here, among them the southern watermeal, one of the world's smallest flowering plants, and the primeval-looking pileated woodpecker.

Viewing Information: Marked nature trails within the preserve are open year-round to foot traffic and to cross-country skiing in the winter. Paved roads throughout the camping area of the park and boating on Lake Renwick diversify viewing opportunities. Spring, summer, and fall are the best seasons for viewing.

Directions: *From Cavalier, go five miles west on North Dakota Highway 5 to the park entrance.*

Ownership: NDPT (265-4561)
Size: 1,000 acres   **Closest Town:** Cavalier

Icelandic State Park features a variety of plant communities. Its woodlands, meadows, and wetland thickets are home to a host of native wildlife species.

5 | CAVALIER WOODS

Description: A statuesque oak woodland, among the few intact stands outside the sand plains and the Pembina Hills. Dominated by mature bur oaks, the woodland has an abundance of edible plants, providing habitat for many species of songbirds.

Viewing Information: A foot trail winds through the woods, beginning and ending at Cavalier municipal park. In winter the trail is used for cross-country skiing. Binoculars are useful for viewing birds in the trees.

Directions: In Cavalier, turn north on 2nd Street North; continue over the bridge to the city park. The trail through Cavalier Woods begins at the north end of the park.

Ownership: City of Cavalier (265-8188)
Size: Thirty-five acres   **Closest Town:** Cavalier

6 | ELMWOOD

Description: A small area of natural forest and river bottom along the Park River at the north edge of the city of Grafton. The forest is the easternmost cottonwood stand in North Dakota, along with box elder and green ash. Wild berry bushes provide food for songbirds such as northern orioles, rose-breasted grosbeaks, and least flycatchers.

Viewing Information: A self-guided walking trail takes you through the area; a trail brochure available at the site points out significant plants. Binoculars will prove helpful in viewing from the trail. The area is open year-round.

Directions: From U.S. 81 at the north end of Grafton, turn east on 3rd Street. Go one block (over railroad tracks) to Wakeman Avenue. Go one block north on Wakeman Ave. to 2nd Street, and turn east to the entrance of Elmwood.

Ownership: NDPT, but contact Grafton Chamber of Commerce (352-0781)
Size: Seven acres   **Closest Town:** Grafton

Bird watchers come from all over the world to see and hear the Baird's sparrow and Sprague's pipit, two rare grassland birds.

7 FOREST RIVER BIOLOGY AREA

Description: Area contains wooded ravines, a segment of the Forest River, a spring-fed creek, and former cropland. Some 425 species of plants have been identified here, providing browse and cover for white-tailed deer, food and cover for snowshoe hares, nesting cover for wood ducks in spring, and habitat for a variety of songbirds. Beaver have dammed the creek, forming a swamp.

Viewing Information: There are walking trails through the area. Dirt roads and trails to the area can be muddy in wet weather and may be impassable. Best seasons for viewing are late spring and summer for wildflowers and songbirds, spring for nesting birds, and fall for deer and beaver.

Directions: From the junction of North Dakota 18 and Grand Forks County Road 1 just east of the town of Inkster, go three miles west on County Road 1. Turn north on the township road .5 mile, then east on a field road for several hundred feet, and finally north around a ravine for about .25 mile.

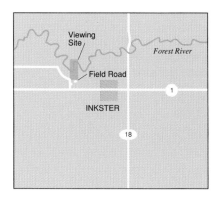

Ownership: UND (777-2621)
Size: 160 acres
Closest Town: Inkster

Yellow-headed blackbirds are most common north and east of the Missouri River. Look for them in marshy areas with cattails or bulrushes.
LYNN BENDER

22

Description: Two large shallow lakes separated by a road. At one time a single lake, these two lakes today feature distinctly different habitats. West Stump Lake has extensive beds of sago pondweed, the most important food for breeding waterfowl in North Dakota, and thus attracts much larger numbers of waterfowl during fall migrations. East Stump Lake features more shorebirds. West Stump Lake is perhaps the best area in the state for viewing staging canvasback ducks in the fall. Tundra swans and snow geese also seen here. Shorebirds to look for are avocets, willets, marbled godwits, and Wilson's phalaropes and migrating sandpipers.

Viewing Information: Most of the land surrounding the two lakes is privately owned; viewing is limited to opportunities from the county road. Viewing from the road between the two lakes is best, especially in years when the water level in the lakes is high. Binoculars are a must.

Directions: *From Lakota, go eight miles south on North Dakota 1. Turn west on Nelson County Road 4 and go two miles to the lakes.*

Ownership: PVT
Size: 3,000 acres
Closest Town: Lakota

The photogenic burrowing owl, more active during the day than at night, can frequently be seen in prairie dog towns.

9 TURTLE RIVER STATE PARK

Description: An area of surprising habitat diversity within the intensively farmed Red River Valley. The forest and adjoining upland along the winding Turtle River provide a home for white-tailed deer, moose, squirrels, and chipmunks. The area is good for songbirds and raptors such as red-tailed hawks and great horned owls in the spring, summer, and fall. There are painted turtles in the river, and children often entertain themselves netting chub minnows.

Viewing Information: Viewing is good along the paved roads throughout the park, especially in early spring and in fall. The park has self-guided nature trails through the forest and along the grassland, and, when it is completed in June of 1992, will offer a self-guided nature trail accessible to wheelchairs. In winter there are marked cross-country ski trails.

Directions: *From Grand Forks, go west twenty-two miles on U.S. 2 to the park entrance on the north side of the highway.*

Ownership: NDPT (594-4445)
Size: 900 acres   **Closest Town:** Arvilla

Ruby-throated hummingbirds are North Dakota's only breeding hummingbird. Look for them mid-summer in the brushy margins and openings in forested areas.
The tiny birds find red flowering plants especially attractive. HAROLD UMBER

10 KELLY'S SLOUGH NATIONAL WILDLIFE REFUGE

Description: A complex of upland grasslands and wetland habitats managed for waterfowl and wildlife production. In the Red River Valley, this is a premier area for viewing migratory and breeding waterfowl. Typical species are mallards, gadwalls, pintails, blue-winged teal, Canada geese, wood ducks, shovelers, redheads, and ruddy ducks. Others species of interest are American bittern, American avocet, great blue herons, black- crowned night herons, and in winter, snowy owls. There is a resident population of white-tailed deer.

Viewing Information: The area around Kelly's Slough NWR will only get better for viewing as time goes on. At present the site is a mixture of refuge land, waterfowl production areas, and easement refuge lands which are privately owned. Best viewing is from the bridge on the north-south gravel road which leads to the refuge from U.S. 2, or by hiking the old railway bed which crosses the refuge southeast to northwest, or by hiking the waterfowl production areas on either side of the gravel road north of the refuge. WPAs are clearly marked with green and white signs. Roads to Kelly's Slough are good gravel, and are passable except in very wet weather. The site is a year-round opportunity for seeing a great variety of birds, but the most active times are during the spring and fall migrations.

Directions: *From the junction of Interstate 29 and U.S. 2 in Grand Forks, go 7.5 miles west on U.S. 2, and 3.3 miles north on the gravel road to the bridge. The railroad bed is a short distance farther north, and the WPAs another .7 mile north. Park anywhere along the gravel road, but be sure to pull off the traveled portion of the road.*

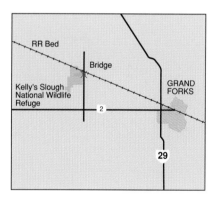

Ownership: USFWS (662-8611)
Size: NWR, 1,620 acres; WPAs, 1,120 acres
Closest Town: Grand Forks

Giant Canada geese, once found only in domestic flocks, have made a comeback and are one of the more common species of breeding waterfowl in North Dakota.

11 LINCOLN PARK AND RIVERSIDE PARK

Description: Walking or cross-country ski trails in two wooded parks along the Red River in the town of Grand Forks. The forest is mixed elm, ash, cottonwood, hackberry, and box elder. The trails within the parks are open to the public; outside the park boundaries, the trails are on private land.

Viewing Information: Bird watching along the trail is good in all seasons, so bring your binoculars. Wood ducks and blue-winged teal can be seen along the river bank spring through fall. Look for eastern cottontails year-round, and fox and gray squirrels in all seasons except mid-winter. Great horned owls hulk in the trees. Occasionally white-tailed deer use the park, and there has been a report of a moose.

Directions: *To Lincoln Park: Take the 32nd Avenue exit from Interstate 29 and go east on 32nd Ave. to Belmont Road. Go north on Belmont to Elks Drive. Take Elks Drive west to Lincoln Park. To Riverside Park: Take the Gateway exit from Interstate 29 and take Gateway east two miles to North 1st Street. Turn left on 1st Street and go five blocks to Riverside Park.*

Ownership: Grand Forks Park District (746-2750)
Size: Lincoln Park, 125 acres; Riverside Park, fifty acres
Closest Town: Grand Forks

Blue jays are common inhabitants of wooded sites such as Lincoln and Riverside parks. This colorful, raucous bird is also a favorite visitor to winter bird feeders across the state. WILLIAM K. VINJE

Description: An impoundment on the Rush River, with food plots, tree plantings, and backwater wetlands. Site is known locally as a wintering area for white-tailed deer and provides habitat for pheasants, gray partridge, and many songbirds. Wetlands serve as brood-rearing habitat for ducks and geese and as staging water for migrating waterfowl. Beaver, fox, and mink can be viewed here. On the southeast corner of the area, thirty-five species of trees have been planted in identified rows.

Viewing Information: Movement within the site is restricted to foot travel. There are some trails. The site is accessible by gravel roads which run along three sides. Best seasons for viewing ducks and other water birds are spring through summer and the migration periods—April and May and again in September through October.

Directions: *From Interstate 29 north of Fargo, take exit 86 and go west 19.5 miles. Turn south and go four miles (through the town of Erie). Turn west and go one mile to the site.*

Ownership: NDGF (683-4900)
Size: 1,031 acres   **Closest Town:** Erie

A typical red fox "family" consists of an adult male and female and a litter of pups. Occasionally there are extra adults, either male or female. LYNN BENDER

13 OAK GROVE PARK

Description: A wooded park trail along a sharp oxbow in the Red River at the north end of the city of Fargo. Most of the park has been cleared of undergrowth, but there are pockets of dense habitat.

Viewing Information: This park is an excellent site for bird watching throughout the year. Songbirds such as warblers, flycatchers, thrushes, vireos, and other passerines fill the park, especially in mid-May. In and along the river look for ducks and herons. Several species of owls may be viewed during the year—long-eared owls in early spring and late fall, eastern screech owls in spring and summer, and great horned owls year-round. Watch for hawks throughout the park.

Directions: *From Interstate 29, take the 12th Avenue North exit to 4th Street North. Go south on 4th Street North to 6th Avenue North, then go east on 6th Avenue North (which turns into South Terrace) until you reach the park gate.*

Ownership: Fargo Park District (241-1350)
Size: Thirty-six acres   **Closest Town:** Fargo

14 LINDENWOOD PARK

Description: Similar to Oak Grove Park, this site offers a wooded walk along the Red River in the city of Fargo. The walking/bike path follows an oxbow in the river under a high canopy of trees with occasional areas of undergrowth.

Viewing Information: Wildlife viewing in Lindenwood Park is best during the songbird migration in April and May. The peak of the migration comes in mid-May and features warblers, vireos, flycatchers, orioles, grosbeaks, and buntings. In spring and fall, waterfowl can be seen in and along the river, with migratory hawks in the tall trees.

Directions: *In Fargo, take Interstate 29 to 17th Avenue South. Go east on 17th Avenue South to 5th Street.*

Ownership: Fargo Park District (241-1350)
Size: Ninety acres   **Closest Town:** Fargo

 Bluebirds are making a comeback in North Dakota thanks to people providing nest boxes. Watch for the boxes and the birds as you travel through the state.

15 HAMILTON WILLS WMA

Description: An area of woodland, brush, and grassland ridges straddling the Maple River. Major species to look for are white-tailed deer, upland birds such as pheasants, wild turkeys, and gray partridge, and wood ducks.

Viewing Information: This Wildlife Management Area is scenic and fairly remote for the Red River Valley, with woods and a few old buildings from a turn-of-the-century town. White-tailed deer can be viewed year-round in the woods along the river. Look for snapping turtles in the river. Wood duck houses have been put up in the area and are used by ducks and wrens. The trees and lower brush are full of songbirds, starting with the spring migration in May. Dutch elm disease has taken its toll on the trees, but raccoons, bluebirds, and woodpeckers have found habitat in the dead ones. Pheasants and wild turkeys can be seen year-round.

Directions: *From Enderlin, go east on North Dakota 46 for ten miles. Turn north and go four miles to the WMA.*

Ownership: NDGF (683-4900)
Size: 480 acres   **Closest Town:** Leonard

The long-eared owl is rare in most of North Dakota. They can be distinguished from the more common great-horned owl by close-set ear tufts, smaller size, and more slender shape.

SHERM SPOELSTRA

29

16 MUEHLER PRAIRIE

Description: A small area of gently rolling tallgrass prairie—a relict of the landscape that greeted the state's first settlers. The site has many resident bobolinks and meadowlarks, typical birds of the prairie, and many butterflies. Colorful wildflowers bloom from June through haying time.

Viewing Information: This site is privately owned. Landowner permission is required for access to the property. Foot travel only will be permitted. The best times to come here are in June, in the first flush of summer, through August, before haying. August is the most colorful, when blazing star and wild sunflowers are in bloom.

Directions: *The landowner screens the number of visitors to protect the fragile prairie ecosystem. Please call the phone number below to request access and obtain directions to the site.*

Ownership: PVT (474-5480)
Size: Eighty acres   **Closest Town:** Hankinson

Rich, dark soil and dependable rainfall made tallgrass prairie the most productive farmland. Only small scattered tracts of this once-lush landscape remain.
BONNIE HEIDEL

REGION TWO:
COTEAUS AND PRAIRIES

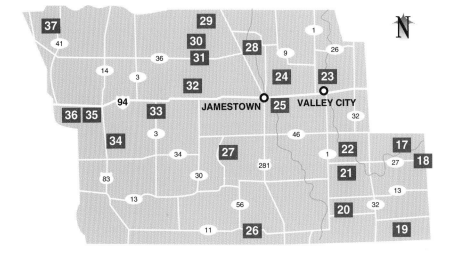

SITE 17 MIRROR POOL WILDLIFE MANAGEMENT AREA	**SITE 28** ARROWWOOD NATIONAL WILDLIFE REFUGE
SITE 18 SHEYENNE NATIONAL GRASSLAND	**SITE 29** HAWKSNEST RIDGE
SITE 19 TEWAUKON NATIONAL WILDLIFE REFUGE	**SITE 30** BARNES LAKE WATERFOWL PRODUCTION AREA
SITE 20 KRAFT SLOUGH	**SITE 31** WOODWORTH WILDLIFE STATION CIRCLE TOUR
SITE 21 ENGLEVALE SLOUGH WILDLIFE MANAGEMENT AREA	**SITE 32** CHASE LAKE NATIONAL WILDLIFE REFUGE
SITE 22 SHEYENNE RIVER VALLEY	**SITE 33** DAWSON WILDLIFE MANAGEMENT AREA
SITE 23 VALLEY CITY NATIONAL FISH HATCHERY	**SITE 34** LONG LAKE NATIONAL WILDLIFE REFUGE
SITE 24 NATIONAL AUDUBON SOCIETY ALKALI LAKE SANCTUARY	**SITE 35** MCKENZIE SLOUGH WMA & WPA
SITE 25 FRONTIER VILLAGE	**SITE 36** SMALL WATERFOWL PRODUCTION AREA
SITE 26 JOHNSON'S GULCH WILDLIFE MANAGEMENT AREA	**SITE 37** KOENIG WILDLIFE DEVELOPMENT AREA
SITE 27 MOLDENHAUER WATERFOWL PRODUCTION AREA	

17 MIRROR POOL WILDLIFE MANAGEMENT AREA

Description: Three tracts of land clustered along four miles of the Sheyenne River, surrounded by grass-covered sand hills. Mirror Pool WMA 1 is the largest tract, featuring a fishing hole, extensive sand dunes, a forest of stately basswood and elm trees, and a series of springs and seeps, all providing habitat for wildlife. Mirror Pool WMA 2, with dense alder and bog birch, is choice habitat for moose. Mirror Pool WMA 3 features an oxbow pool with turtles and beaver, and a path that climbs through sandhill prairie to a scenic overview of the Sheyenne River Valley. The three tracts provide habitat for deer, turkeys, woodcocks, waterfowl, and a variety of songbirds. Wood, leopard, and tree frogs are also found here.

Viewing Information: The sites offer year-round viewing opportunities, especially for deer and turkeys. Viewing of songbirds, reptiles, and amphibians is best in summer; waterfowl opportunities are best in spring and fall. Mirror Pool WMA 2 is moose habitat, but don't expect to see them from the edge of the dense tangle of brush. Best viewing in WMAs 1 and 3 is by hiking or riding horseback along the trails which wind through the tracts. Mirror Pool WMA can be difficult to get to during the winter and after heavy rains.

Directions: To Mirror Pool WMA 1, follow North Dakota 46 east fourteen miles from Enderlin. Turn south and go four miles, then west one mile, south one mile, and finally southeast on a prairie trail. For directions to Mirror Pool WMAs 2 and 3, contact the Game and Fish Office in Lisbon. Please note: the road may be muddy
after a rain, and the prairie trail to Mirror Pool 1 might be impassable. Visitors to this area will find a U.S. Forest Service map of the Sheyenne National Grassland (available at the Forest Service district office in Lisbon) very useful in finding these sites.

Ownership: NDGF (683-4900)
Size: 400 acres
Closest Town: McLeod or Lisbon

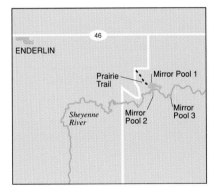

Due to the climate, North Dakota has only twenty-eight species of reptiles and amphibians, one of the smallest totals in the United States.

Description: A large area, the unifying feature of which is a thick mantle of sand deposited by advancing glacial ice. The northern end of the National Grassland is oak savanna—rolling prairie dotted with groves of bur oak. Along the Sheyenne River are hardwood forests of basswood, American elm, and green ash. The main portion of the grassland is prairie. The National Grassland provides a home to wildflowers like prairie smoke, western wallflower, spiderwort, penstemon, and hairy puccoon. The wildflowers in turn attract a beautiful array of butterflies, among them the regal fritillary and the Dakota skipper. The grassland is North Dakota's only stronghold for the greater prairie chicken.

Viewing Information: April is the best month to view the greater prairie chicken as male birds display on booming grounds. The U.S. Forest Service sets up an observation blind for public use— stop in at the district office in Lisbon for directions and schedules. Turkeys and white-tailed deer can be seen in early morning and late evening May through October. Migratory songbirds such as warblers, vireos, meadowlarks, bluebirds, orioles, and sparrows abound in the spring. A twenty-five-mile portion of the North Country National Scenic Trail crosses the area, and provides good opportunities to see its varied wildlife.

Directions: *There are two trailheads for the North Country Trail. One is located three miles south of North Dakota 27 on Ransom County Road 54. The other is located 6.5 miles north of North Dakota 27 on Richland County Road 23. The trail is marked by blue diamonds and is designated for non-motorized use only. For information about the prairie chicken observation blind and for maps and other information, stop in at the U.S. Forest Service district office at 701 Main Street in Lisbon.*

Ownership: USFS (683-4342)
Size: 71,000 acres   **Closest Town:** Lisbon

Oak savannah is one of many habitats in the Sheyenne National Grassland. The partially-wooded savannah is home to white-tailed deer, gray squirrels, blue jays, brown thrashers, common flickers, and red-tailed hawks.

CRAIG BIHRLE

19 TEWAUKON NATIONAL WILDLIFE REFUGE

Description: A series of natural and manmade lakes and marshes which serve as a staging area for migrating snow and blue geese and for a wide variety of ducks during spring and fall. Wetlands and grasslands on the site are managed to meet the seasonal needs of waterfowl. These, along with some small scattered areas of trees, provide habitat for waterfowl, shorebirds, songbirds, and white-tailed deer. A total of 243 species of birds have been identified on the refuge. A fair range of small mammals and predators can also be seen, including red fox, mink, raccoon, skunk, muskrat, beaver, badger, weasel, ground squirrel, and an occasional coyote.

Viewing Information: Thousands of migrating and nesting waterfowl are on the refuge in the spring and fall. Spring, summer, and fall are good seasons for viewing other birds, and whitetails and red fox can be seen year-round. The refuge around Lake Tewaukon (east of County Road 12) is open to hiking, and roads on the east side of County Road 12 are open to vehicles except during hunting season. Boats with motors no larger than twenty-five horsepower are allowed on Lake Tewaukon. Stop at the refuge headquarters to get a map, wildlife checklists, and information about other activities. The refuge is open from dawn to 10:00 p.m. daily, and the headquarters is open 8:00 a.m. to 4:30 p.m. Monday through Friday.

Directions: *Take North Dakota 11 to the junction with Sargent County Road 12 at Cayuga. Go south on County Road 12 five miles to the refuge entrance.*

Ownership: USFWS (724-3598)
Size: 8,438 acres   **Closest Town:** Cayuga

In the spring of 1991, open water on Lake Tewaukon coincided with the major goose migration to produce an unusual and spectacular concentration of snow geese, Canada geese, and white-fronted geese. Estimated numbers ran as high as 700,000 birds.
DAPHNE KINZLER

Description: A large area of wetlands surrounded by grassland. The topography varies from flat on the northeast end to rolling hills at the southwest. The site is one of the few tracts in North Dakota that contains relatively undisturbed biotic communities. Bird diversity is high—breeding records include 176 species.

Viewing Information: The area is excellent for viewing snow and blue geese during the spring and fall migrations. Spring and summer are good times to see black-crowned night herons and great blue herons. Ducks such as pintails, mallards, gadwalls, and redheads breed here and can be viewed spring, summer, and fall. At the southwest end of the area a high hill provides an overlook of the open water in the wetland. Bring your binoculars. Much of the area is in private land, and viewing is limited to what can be seen from the county road. The site is in the process of being developed; additional viewing opportunities will become available over time. Contact the Bureau of Reclamation office in Bismarck for more information.

Directions: *From Cogswell go west 5.5 miles on North Dakota 11 to the junction with Sargent County Road 2. Go north one mile on County Road 2 and circle to an overlook of the wetland below.*

Ownership: PVT/BOR (250-4721)
Size: 1,310 acres
Closest Town: Cogswell

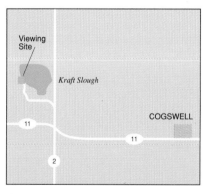

North Dakota's large wetlands such as Kraft Slough provide critical staging areas for snow geese during the fall and spring migrations. The fat the birds build up here must sustain them for the long flights north in spring and south in fall.

DAPHNE KINZLER

21 ENGLEVALE SLOUGH WMA AND WPA

Description: A four-mile by .25-mile wetland surrounded by grassland and marshes. The area was once the southern flow route of glacial melt into glacial Lake Dakota. Today's wetland marsh and surrounding upland serves as a resting area for migrating and nesting ducks and geese, and is good habitat for pelicans, herons, sharp-tailed grouse, pheasants, gray partridge, and white-tailed deer.

Viewing Information: Waterfowl activity at the site is water-dependent. In a wet spring, the site is very reliable for Canada geese and dabbling ducks like mallards and gadwalls. It is a year-round site for white-tailed deer and upland birds. There are gravel roads on the west and south edges of the slough, and a trail on the east side. The east-west gravel road at the south edge of the site offers a good vista, as does the trail on the east side. Feel free to hike over the Wildlife Management Area and the Waterfowl Production areas.

Directions: *From Lisbon, go twelve miles west on North Dakota 27 to the trail on the east side of the area, or thirteen miles to the gravel road on the west side. Turn south on either road.*

Ownership: NDGF (683-4900); USFWS (647-2866)
Size: WMA, 160 acres; WPA, 1,900 acres   **Closest Town:** Englevale

The Sheyenne River flows through a valley which was once a meltwater channel feeding a glacial lake. The river flows through diverse habitats—sand dunes, prairies, and hardwood forests, making it rich in viewing opportunities. KEITH KRAMER

Description: A scenic river and valley offering varied recreation and viewing opportunities. Fort Ransom State Park and the Sheyenne State Forest lie along the Sheyenne River with its hardwood forest dominated by elm, green ash, and oak. Fort Ransom State Park also has large areas of open grassland, some of which has been restored to native prairie. Both white-tailed deer and wild turkeys are abundant in the river valley. Wood ducks nest here in the spring and raise their broods in the summer. Small mammals like ground squirrels attract northern harriers and red-tailed hawks. More than fifty species of songbirds have been identified here as well as thirty species of wildflowers.

Viewing Information: Viewing opportunities abound. A drive along the road following the river (between Lisbon and North Dakota 46) early in the morning or in the evening is usually good for viewing deer and turkeys. The park and the state forest have self-guided walking trails with brochures available at the sites. The Sheyenne River is one of North Dakota's best opportunities for wildlife viewing by canoe—Fort Ransom State Park offers a canoe trail, canoe access to the river, and canoe rentals. In winter, the park and the State Forest are good for cross-country skiing. Camping is available at the park, and there is a fee for use of park facilities.

Directions: *From Lisbon, go .5 mile north on North Dakota 32 and turn west on the gravel road on the north side of the river. This scenic route (about twenty-five miles) follows the river past the Sheyenne State Forest and Fort Ransom State Park northwest to North Dakota 46.*

Ownership: NDFS (683-4323) and NDPT (973-4331)
Size: Twenty-five-mile scenic drive, 500 acres of state forest, and 900 acres of state park
Closest Town: Fort Ransom

The pocket gopher is the only true gopher in North Dakota, but there are three ground squirrels that people mistakenly call gophers.

23 VALLEY CITY NATIONAL FISH HATCHERY

Description: A fish hatchery and two rearing pond units along the wooded Sheyenne River below Baldhill Dam. The main hatchery, visitor center, and lower rearing ponds are three miles northwest of Valley City; the upper ponds are seven miles farther upstream. The river bottom forest is elm, oak, and ash, with brush and shrubs such as lilac and chokecherry. Wildlife species in this mixture of habitat are Canada geese, ducks, herons, bitterns, terns, cormorants, pelicans, and wild turkeys. There are white-tailed deer, squirrels, fox, and coyote. Fish can be viewed in the rearing ponds or in the hatchery.

Viewing Information: Spring is the best season to visit the site for waterfowl and most other birds. Canada geese begin to arrive in April and stay through the summer. The picnic area is often a good place to view geese. Wood ducks nest at the site, and other ducks remain through the migration period. Bitterns, herons, and terns can be viewed around the warm-water rearing ponds, again, mainly in spring. In the wooded areas and along the road between the two units, look for white-tailed deer and turkeys in the early morning and at dusk. A feeder at the west end of the hatchery attracts deer and birds. You can walk along the pond dike roads (no vehicle access) and view fish in the ponds. The hatchery's visitor center offers a more complete view of hatchery activities.

Directions: From Valley City, go north three miles on Barnes County Road 17.

Ownership: USFWS (845-3464)
Size: 71.5 acres   **Closest Town:** Valley City

Cavity-nesting wood ducks have increased in North Dakota, largely due to their willingness to use artificial nesting boxes. Among the best places to view them are Arrowwood National Wildlife Refuge, along the Sheyenne River near the Valley City National Fish Hatchery, and the Forest River Biology Area. C. D. GRONDAHL

24 NATIONAL AUDUBON SOCIETY ALKALI LAKE SANCTUARY

Description: Nearly 2,000 acres of grasslands and wooded shoreline surrounding a 500-acre lake. Sanctuary lands were once cropped or grazed but have been restored to native prairie or dense nesting cover for wildlife. The lake and smaller wetlands on the sanctuary are being managed and restored to provide waterfowl nesting habitat and feeding and resting areas for migrating birds. There are opportunities here to view many of the other species typical of a prairie ecosystem.

Viewing Information: Viewing opportunities abound in the sanctuary. Make arrangements beforehand with the sanctuary manager. Although you can view wildlife from township and section-line roads around the site, it's better to park your car by the pole barn at the entrance to the sanctuary and walk the trails. The roads can be muddy, and might be impassable to low-clearance vehicles. Geese and ducks are on the lake or feeding on nearby uplands during spring, summer, and fall. White pelicans can be seen most of the summer. From blinds you can watch and photograph sharp-tailed grouse on their dancing grounds in the spring and water birds on the lake. The sanctuary manager will also be able to guide you to particularly good or unusual viewing opportunities—be sure to ask.

Directions: *From Jamestown, go north on North Dakota 20 to the eight-mile marker. Turn east and go four miles to the entrance to the sanctuary.*

Ownership: National Audubon Society (252-3822)
Size: 2,250 acres   **Closest Town:** Jamestown

25 FRONTIER VILLAGE

Description: A fenced wooded ravine and upland grassland featuring a small herd of bison.

Viewing Information: A picnic area overlooks the buffalo pasture. The small herd of bison will be allowed to increase to thirty or thirty-five animals. It may also be possible to spot nesting wood ducks in the spring and summer, and gray partridge on the uplands. These are difficult to see, so bring your binoculars. Restrooms and other facilities at the site are open only in summer.

Directions: *From Interstate 94, take the U.S. 281 exit and go north to 17th Street South (Louis Lamour Road). Turn right, and proceed to Frontier Village and the "World's Largest Buffalo."*

Ownership: North Dakota Buffalo Foundation (251-2265)
Size: 125 acres   **Closest Town:** Jamestown

26 | JOHNSON'S GULCH WILDLIFE MANAGEMENT AREA

Description: A large, deep, wooded ravine, smaller ravines, and areas of prairie grasses. A spring-fed creek winds through the bottom of Johnson's Gulch. The steep landscape of the ravines was formed by glacial meltwater as it ran off the huge mounds of debris piled by the leading edge of the advancing glacier. The relatively level land to the east was ground flat by the ice sheet. An area which once fed bison—bison bones can be seen embedded in the creek banks at the bottom of the gulch—now feeds white-tailed deer, red fox, and coyote. Songbirds nest in the oak and green ash forest in the spring.

Viewing Information: The only way to view wildlife in Johnson's Gulch is on foot. There are two parking areas on the wildlife management area, one at the gulch and another to the east on the level grassland. The best opportunity for viewing wildlife is in the gulch at the western end of the WMA. The road to the parking area at the gulch is steep and eroded—low-clearance vehicles should use caution. Trails within the gulch are also steep. Camping is allowed in the management area, and there are primitive campsites and outdoor toilets. If you plan to stay longer than ten days, a permit is required.

Directions: *From the junction of North Dakota 11 and North Dakota 56, go .7 mile east, then turn onto the gravel road and proceed 4.5 miles south and east to the entrance of the wildlife management area. Circle around the monument, and go down into the parking area. Use caution—the road is steep and eroded, and can be muddy.*

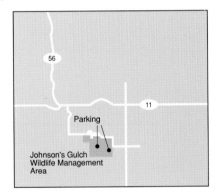

Ownership: NDGF (683-4900)
Size: 1,400 acres
Closest Town: Ellendale

The coyote is the most common predator in North Dakota and can be found almost statewide.

27 MOLDENHAUER WATERFOWL PRODUCTION AREA

Description: Rolling grassland surrounding a wetland complex. Species to look for in spring are dabbling ducks such as mallards, gadwalls, and pintails, and divers such as redheads and canvasbacks in breeding plumage. Canada geese nest here. Spring is the best time for viewing lesser yellowlegs and upland sandpipers, and fall for upland game birds. After freeze-up, look for golden eagles and bald eagles.

Viewing Information: Access to the WPA by car is limited to the roads and parking areas, but you can walk anywhere you want. There are two parking areas, one on the north side, accessible from the gravel road, and the other on the south side, accessible from the dirt road into the WPA. In winter or in wet weather, park in the area on the north side and walk. As soon as the ice is off in spring (early April), Canada geese can be seen on nesting bales from the hills on the north side of the site—bring your binoculars or a good spotting scope. May is good for watching hatched broods of geese; June and July are good for ducks. During late September and October there is a tremendous build-up of ducks and geese as the fall migration moves through the area. A high hill in the southwest corner of the area gives a good overlook of the whole marsh.

Directions: From Gackle, take North Dakota 56 south for 6.5 miles. Turn east on the gravel road and proceed 1.5 miles to the north parking area or two miles to the dirt road that leads to the south parking area.

Ownership: USFWS (647-2866)
Size: 600 acres   **Closest Town:** Gackle

In 1988, a pair of bald eagles successfully nested and fledged an eaglet—the first time this had happened in the state since the turn of the century. Most often, bald eagles are migrants or winter residents in North Dakota.
SHERM SPOELSTRA

41

PRAIRIE POTHOLES

The small lakes, ponds, and wetlands of North Dakota's prairie pothole region were formed by moving and melting ice age glaciers. Potholes are essentially depressions in the ground that collect water. They are mostly shallow and often temporary, but they are full of life. The pothole region has evolved into a complex ecosystem which contains—or produces—everything necessary for the plants and animals that live and breed there.

In the spring, melting snow and spring rain fill the potholes. Sun and water start an explosion of plant, insect, and animal life. The pothole environment has been described as a factory for food and cover, with many species of plants and animals adapted to its yearly cycle. Ducks are a prime example.

By the time ducks reach the pothole country in spring, most are already paired for breeding. The explosion of life in thawing potholes provides the birds with rich food to recover from the stress of migration and, for hens, the nutrition necessary for egg-laying. After a period of feeding and mating, hens select a nest site in dense protective cover around a pothole or in nearby uplands. During the egg-laying and incubation period, hens leave

North Dakota's duck "factory": the prairie pothole region.
WILLIAM K. VINJE

their nests to feed at the potholes. After a twenty-six day incubation, the eggs hatch, and hens lead their broods to a pothole's open water. There, the ducklings can feed and grow in the relative safety of cover and open water until they are able to fly. Ducks thus depend on prairie potholes from the time they arrive in spring until they leave in fall.

The prairie pothole region is a highly productive ecosystem. The breeding behavior of ducks has, over time, become adapted to the yearly cycle of melting, explosive growth, and slow drying of prairie potholes. The close match between the cycle of the potholes and the needs of ducks is not a coincidence. Ducks are only one example of how plant and animal life have become interdependent within ecosystems. Changes in the prairie pothole region may have consequences far beyond waterfowl—something to consider when we talk about conservation.

Mallards are typical "puddle ducks" of the pothole region. The shallow, seasonal, and often temporary wetlands provide food and dense cover for nesting and brood rearing. C. S. NIELSEN

28 ARROWWOOD NATIONAL WILDLIFE REFUGE

Description: A large area of marshes, grasslands, cultivated fields and wooded ravines clustered around shallow impoundments along the James River. The site attracts good numbers of snow and Canada geese during spring and fall migrations, and is a prime nesting area for blue-winged teal, mallards, gadwalls, and wood ducks. The uplands are home to sharp-tailed grouse, gray partridge, and ring-necked pheasant. The wooded ravines are filled with white-tailed deer.

Viewing Information: A 5.5-mile self-guided auto tour winds through both prairie and marsh. Brochures for the tour are available at the tour entrance. In April and early May, the refuge sets up an observation blind for dancing sharp-tailed grouse. The blind is open to the public by reservation. Visitors can walk anywhere on the refuge, and the picnic area is popular for birding. The best times for viewing geese and tundra swans is October; ducks, April through October; grouse and white-tailed deer, year- round. Deer are often on the auto tour road during twilight hours, so be careful. Parts of the refuge are open to hunting during the seasons. Stop at the headquarters to find out about these and other activities taking place at the site.

Directions: *From Edmunds, go .5 mile north on U.S. 281, then turn east on Stutsman County Road 44. Go five miles to the refuge headquarters.*

Ownership: USFWS (285-3341)
Size: 15,934 acres   **Closest Town:** Pingree

American bitterns favor marsh habitat with dense, reedy vegetation. Long Lake National Wildlife Refuge, Kelly's Slough, and Turtle Mountain sites such as Lake Metigoshe State Park offer excellent opportunities to view them.
LYNN BENDER

Traditional whitetail range in North Dakota was in riverbottom forest like the cottonwood forest of the Missouri. Since the late 1940s, white-tailed deer have expanded into all parts of North Dakota, showing adaptability to new habitat and food sources. D. ROBERT FRANZ   45

29 HAWKSNEST RIDGE

Description: The highest point in a short ridge of glacial moraine hills. Hawksnest rises 800 feet above the surrounding prairie; from the top it is possible to see thirty miles in all directions. The site was sacred to prehistoric native cultures. It is a woodland area with oak, elm, aspen, box elder, and ash trees, and an underbrush of chokecherry, plum, juneberry, and wolfberry. The area offers good cover and a ready food supply for year-round residents such as white-tailed deer, sharp-tailed grouse, gray partridge, and pheasants. Many small mammals—rabbits, mink, badgers, squirrels, weasels, and raccoons, and predators such as coyotes and foxes—live here.

Viewing Information: Wildlife viewing is, at the present time, on foot, although development is planned. There are steep trails through heavily wooded ravines and on gentle slopes. In normal years for moisture, natural springs supply a stream winding through the bottom of the ravines. Most species can be viewed year-round, but it is important to be at the site during early morning or late evening hours when animals are most active. Gates are open twenty-four hours a day. There is primitive camping at the site.

Directions: *From Carrington, go west on North Dakota 200 for six miles to the Wells-Foster county line. Turn south on a the gravel road for 7.5 miles to the entrance to the site.*

Ownership: PVT (Hawksnest Ridge Corporation 652-2362)
Size: 103 acres   **Closest Town:** Carrington

To watch mink, first look for muskrat houses. Muskrats are a primary source of food for mink, and mink often use muskrat burrows as den sites.
C. D. GRONDAHL

Description: A large open lake with some shoreline vegetation and grass uplands on the north and east sides. During the spring migration, the lake draws good numbers of Canada geese, and in the fall, snow geese. Tundra swans are abundant in spring and fall. During the nesting season, the lake can be covered with ducks. The site draws white pelicans in spring and summer, and western grebes and canvasbacks in fall. The area is good for sharp-tailed grouse—historically there has been a spring dancing ground just north of the Waterfowl Production Area. There are fox in the area, especially in spring.

Viewing Information: A gravel road hugs the shoreline around more than half the lake, making waterfowl viewing with binoculars relatively easy from the car. A boat ramp at the picnic area on the northwest shore of the lake gives boating access to a point of land pushing into the southeast part of the lake. This point was once a favorite spot for hunting canvasbacks, and now affords an excellent opportunity to watch them. Ducks—mallards, pintails, gadwalls, blue-winged teal, and others—are in the area mid-April through the summer. The fall build-up comes in late September and early October.

Directions: From North Dakota 36 just north of Woodworth, take the gravel road 5.9 miles north. Turn east on the gravel road that circles the lake. When you park, be sure to pull off the traveled portion of the road.

Ownership: USFWS (285-3341)
Size: 990 acres   **Closest Town:** Woodworth

Tundra swans were once called whistling swans because of their high-pitched call. Barnes Lake is a reliable viewing site, as are Lords Lake and Grahams Island State Park. JAMES F. PARNELL

31 | WOODWORTH WILDLIFE STATION CIRCLE TOUR

Description: An auto/walking tour of the Woodworth Station's experiments in land and wetland management techniques for the benefit of wildlife. The tour points visitors to an old tree claim, favored habitat for white-tailed deer and songbirds; wetlands used as nesting and brood rearing sites for Canada geese; fields planted to dense nesting cover for grouse and ducks; and a privately owned sharp-tailed grouse dancing ground. In addition to wildlife viewing opportunities, the tour interprets the diversity of the prairie-wetland community, a beautiful and very stable environment.

Viewing Information: What you see on the tour depends on when you visit. Grouse dance in late April. Geese and ducks are nesting and rearing broods in the spring and early summer. Deer, along with pheasants and gray partridge, can be seen feeding year-round. Walk anywhere, but keep to the trail with your vehicle. The sharptail dancing ground is on private land—please respect it. The station office is open Monday through Friday, 8:00 a.m. to 4:30 p.m.

Directions: *At the south edge of the town of Woodworth—east of the grain elevator—go east on the gravel road 2.9 miles to the station headquarters. A kiosk with tour brochures is on the southwest side of the headquarters building.*

Ownership: USFWS (752-4218)
Size: 2.5 mile tour   **Closest Town:** Woodworth

Large numbers of pelicans breed at Chase Lake National Wildlife Refuge, though the birds travel all over North Dakota to feed. Tags from fish living in the Little Missouri River have been recovered at Chase Lake—more than one hundred miles away. LYNN BENDER

Description: A large alkali lake with rolling grasslands—characteristic features of the Missouri Coteau region of North Dakota. The primary attractions of the refuge are thousands of white pelicans, gulls, and cormorants that nest here every year. The colony of nesting white pelicans numbers between 10,000 and 12,000 birds, and is the largest in North America. Other species of interest are piping plover, Baird's sparrow, and Sprague's pipit.

Viewing Information: A June evening at Chase Lake is extraordinary as the pelicans, gulls, and cormorants raise their voices from its islands and peninsulas. The peak breeding season for pelicans is mid-April to late July. Access to the islands where the birds nest is not permitted (you can walk anywhere else on the refuge), but the view from Chase Lake Pass—the road between Chase Lake and Fisher Lake immediately northwest—is excellent. For opportunities to see piping plover, Baird's sparrow, and Sprague's pipit, stop in to see the manager at Woodworth Experiment Station (east of Woodworth) or call the number below.

Directions: *From the Medina exit on Interstate 94, go 9.6 miles north on Stutsman County Road 68. Turn west for three miles, north for four miles, west for five miles, and then south for approximately three miles to the access road into Chase Lake NWR.*

Ownership: USFWS (752-4218)
Size: 4,385 acres
Closest Town: Medina

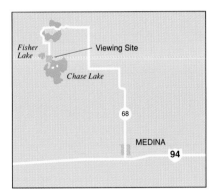

Fisher Lake

Viewing Site

Chase Lake

68

MEDINA

94

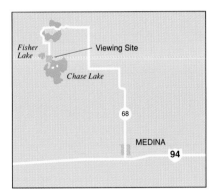
North Dakota's saline wetlands and river sandbars are home to the largest number of breeding piping plovers in the United States.

33 DAWSON WILDLIFE MANAGEMENT AREA

Description: An area of mixed tree belts, grassland, and former cropland. The area is used extensively by white-tailed deer, sharp-tailed grouse, and pheasants.

Viewing Information: This site is especially good for watching deer—it is a key wintering area for deer in the region. You can walk anywhere on the WMA, and primitive camping is permitted. Hunting and trapping are also permitted—be aware of season openings and closings. Further information is available from the Game and Fish Department's office in Bismarck. Roads to the WMA are good gravel, but parking areas may be muddy or full of snow. Poison ivy is abundant.

Directions: From the Dawson exit on Interstate 94, go south on North Dakota 3 for 7.3 miles to the WMA.

Ownership: NDGF (224-3344)
Size: 2,951 acres   **Closest Town:** Dawson

34 LONG LAKE NATIONAL WILDLIFE REFUGE

Description: A long alkali lake in the bed of a pre-glacial river. Some 16,000 acres are lake bottom, with another 6,300 acres of rolling prairie and cultivated uplands. Among migrant birds which visit the refuge in the fall are large numbers of sandhill cranes, Franklin's gulls, and Canada geese. Pintails, blue-winged teal, gadwalls, and mallard ducks nest on the refuge as do American bittern, piping plover, killdeer, and upland plover. The principal upland birds are sharp-tailed grouse, gray partridge, and ring-necked pheasant.

Viewing Information: Franklin's gulls appear in large numbers beginning in late August. View sandhill cranes between mid-September and late October; other migrants stop over throughout the fall. In early spring, the refuge places an observation blind at a sharp-tailed grouse dancing ground—check at the headquarters for its location. There is a picnic shelter on the north side of the refuge—the road on this side can be muddy and slippery in wet weather. Refuge is closed to ground entry except by special arrangement with the refuge manager. Bird watchers and photographers are encouraged to stop at the refuge headquarters. The headquarters is open 7:30 a.m. to 4:00 p.m.; refuge open sunrise to sunset.

Directions: From Moffit, go one mile south, 2.5 miles east, and one mile northeast over the dike to the refuge headquarters.

Ownership: USFWS (387-4397)
Size: 22,300 acres   **Closest Town:** Moffit

35 MCKENZIE SLOUGH WMA & WPA

Description: Intermingled wetlands, grassland, single- and multi-row shelterbelts, and cropland as wildlife food plots. The area is excellent for waterfowl and shorebirds, especially in wet years, and is widely used by waterfowl and upland bird hunters.

Viewing Information: Best viewing is during the spring, when birds are nesting, and in the fall, during the migration period before freeze-up. The reliability of viewing for both the Wildlife Management Area and Waterfowl Production Area depends on water. In wet years, birds are numerous. To increase your opportunities, you might consider a portable blind. There are no roads through the area, but plenty of trails to walk.

Directions: *From Interstate 94, take the McKenzie exit and go south 1.1 miles past where the pavement ends to a parking area on the east side of the road. There is another parking area .5 mile farther south, also on the east side of the road. In wet weather, the parking areas may be soft.*

Ownership: NDGF (224-3344) and USFWS (387-4397)
Size: WMA 682 acres   **Closest Town:** McKenzie

36 SMALL WATERFOWL PRODUCTION AREA

Description: A wetland basin surrounded by woodlands. The wetland area attracts a large variety of waterfowl, wading birds, and shorebirds, especially in the spring and summer. These in turn attract predators like red fox, red-tailed hawks, and great horned owls. Deer use the area for cover during fawning and winter. The U.S. Fish and Wildlife Service and the local wildlife club and Boy Scout troop are cooperating to improve the site for wildlife. They have mowed a walking trail and put up interpretive signs, and are planning an observation deck. The trail has two loops, one .75 mile long, and the other, 1.5 miles.

Viewing Information: The value of the area for waterfowl and other aquatic species depends on the amount of water in the basin. During wet years, the reliability of the site for waterfowl is excellent mid-April to August. Raptors, particularly great horned owls and red-tailed hawks, can usually be seen in the woodlands, especially in fall when the leaves are off. White-tailed deer can be seen year-round, particularly in the early morning and twilight hours.

Directions: *Take the Menoken exit from Interstate 94 and go south 1.2 miles to Apple Creek Road. Turn west, and go 3.4 miles to 119 Street SE. A parking area and trailhead are on the northeast corner of the intersection.*

Ownership: USFWS (387-4397)
Size: 285 acres   **Closest Town:** Menoken

37 KOENIG WILDLIFE DEVELOPMENT AREA

Description: Gently rolling tame and native grassland, prairie wetlands, and the McClusky Canal provide habitat, especially for sharp-tailed grouse and pheasants, and wading birds such as American avocets. The area also serves as a migration stopover for yellowlegs, dowitchers, and other shorebirds.

Viewing Information: The site is very reliable for upland birds, especially sharp-tailed grouse in April when male birds congregate on their dancing grounds at sunrise. The peak time for nesting begins in mid-May. Shorebird viewing is best in fall. Automobile viewing is possible from the network of county roads around and through the area; walking access is also permitted. County roads are gravel, and well-maintained. Auto traffic is not allowed on the McClusky Canal right-of-way. There is walking access to the site from a number of places along the county roads which circle the perimeter of the site.

Directions: *From Wilton, go north on North Dakota 41 nineteen miles to McLean County Road 18. Go west five miles on County Road 18, then north one mile. A*

parking area and a gate are immediately east. There are other access points along the perimeter of the site. The land around the site is privately owned; please respect it. Watch for signs that indicate the Wildlife Development Area.

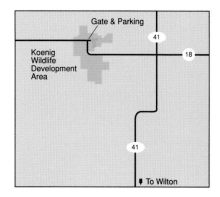

Ownership: USFWS (442-5474)
Size: 3,447 acres
Closest Town: Mercer

American avocets prefer mudflats and sparsely-vegetated shorelines along alkaline and saline ponds and lakes. East Stump Lake and Koenig Wildlife Development Area are reliable sites in North Dakota.
MICHAEL S. SAMPLE

REGION THREE: WEST

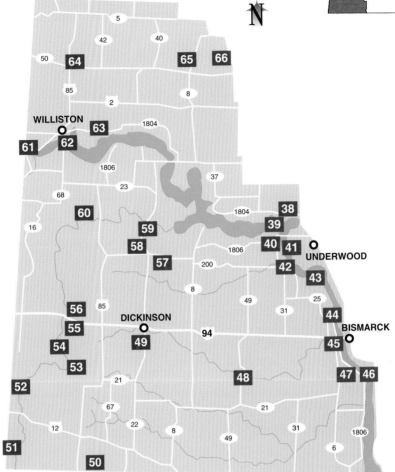

38 CUSTER MINE WILDLIFE MANAGEMENT AREA

Description: Herbaceous and woody cover established on strip mine spoil piles. The site is an example of voluntary attempts to reclaim strip-mined land. Between 150,000 and 200,000 trees have been planted on the site, and wetlands have been developed as a cooperative project between the Game and Fish Department and Ducks Unlimited. The area provides cover for white-tailed deer, Canada geese, and dabbling ducks. Spring and summer feature songbirds and wildflowers.

Viewing Information: The chances of seeing white-tailed deer are excellent year-round. Canada geese, mallards, and gadwalls can be seen in the developed wetlands spring and summer. Viewing towers, trails, and an interpretive brochure are being developed. A paved parking area is immediately adjacent to the site.

Directions: From the town of Garrison, go 5.5 miles east on North Dakota 37 to just west of the junction with U.S. 83.

Ownership: NDGF (654-7475)
Size: 694 acres   **Closest Town:** Garrison

39 FORT STEVENSON STATE PARK

Description: A peninsula of land between two bays of Lake Sakakawea, with gently rolling prairie and shelter belts. The grass provides dense nesting cover for sharp-tailed grouse and ring-necked pheasant. Small mammals at the site include skunks, raccoons, the occasional badger, jackrabbits, and a prairie dog colony at the west end. Canada geese also use the site. You may see coyote or fox.

Viewing Information: Viewing at the park is mostly on foot or by bicycle on developed trails. Nesting Canada geese can be seen along the shoreline spring through summer; the hunting season is also good as geese are flushed out of other areas. Viewing of pheasants and white-tailed deer is best in fall and winter when they are attracted to the area by feeders.

Directions: From Garrison, go south three miles on McLean County Road 15 to the park entrance.

Ownership: NDPT (337-5576)
Size: 600 acres   **Closest Town:** Garrison

40 GARRISON DAM NATIONAL FISH HATCHERY OUTFLOW CHANNEL

Description: The channel for warm water discharged from the National Fish Hatchery at Garrison Dam. The area was once river bottom of the Missouri River. Beaver have dammed the channel, forming a wetland that remains open even after freeze-up because of warm-water discharge. The area gets heavy use from waterfowl that over-winter, and attracts bald and golden eagles and other predators.

Viewing Information: The site is especially good for viewing eagles, great horned owls, and waterfowl during late fall, winter, and early spring when everything else is frozen. The best viewing is at the beaver pond, which you cannot see from the road. Park by the road on the south end of the hatchery and walk west cross-country (there's no marked trail) about 200 yards. Look for a fixed blind at the site for viewing and photography.

Directions: From Riverdale, take North Dakota 200 west over the Garrison Dam spillway (about one mile) and follow the signs toward the downstream campgrounds. Park along the campground road at the south end of the hatchery.

Ownership: USFWS (654-7451)
Size: Twenty acres   **Closest Town:** Riverdale

Coyotes have survived extravagant efforts to get rid of them. They have been in North Dakota for centuries—Lewis and Clark called them "prairie wolves"—but today their range may be larger than ever before. HARRY ENGLES

41 RIVERDALE WILDLIFE MANAGEMENT AREA

Description: Habitat associated with the Missouri River— hardwood forests, hardwood draws, and upland grassland. The area is located where the ranges of eastern and western species of songbirds overlap—more than 100 species of songbirds have been identified here. Site is a wintering area for white-tailed deer and bald eagles, and features a sharp-tailed grouse dancing ground.

Viewing Information: Spring, summer, and early fall are the best seasons to view songbirds at the site as different species migrate through and nest. The best time for viewing white-tailed deer and bald eagles is during the winter when leaves are off the trees and brush. Grouse begin to dance in early April. The Game and Fish Department does not set up an observation blind at this site, but portable blinds are welcome. Contact the Riverdale office of the Game and Fish Department for directions to the dancing ground and for information about grouse activity.

Directions: *From Riverdale, go west on North Dakota 200 to the gravel road just before the Garrison Dam spillway (about .5 mile) and turn south. The road gradually turns west; take the second road which turns south, and go another .5 mile; turn east or west to the WMA.*

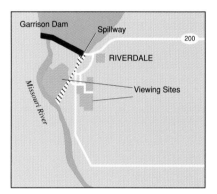

Ownership: COE, managed by NDGF (654-7475)
Size: 2,197 acres
Closest Town: Riverdale

Look for cedar waxwings in berry bushes and fruit trees, especially in spring and summer. The birds have a reputation for erratic behavior after feeding off the fermented berries and fruits of last year's crop.
DAPHNE KINZLER

42 | KNIFE RIVER INDIAN VILLAGES NATIONAL HISTORIC SITE

Description: River bottom and upland grassland associated with the Missouri and Knife Rivers. The river bottom forest is dominated by cottonwood, green ash, box elder, and elm. Brushy species include buffaloberry, chokecherry, and juneberry. The upland terraces have thick stands of native and introduced grasses. The site provides year-round food and cover for white-tailed deer and wild turkeys. Bald eagles winter here. White pelicans visit the site in the spring, and Canada geese pass through on spring and fall migrations. Fewer birds remain throughout the summer.

Viewing Information: The site is named for three Hidatsa Indian earth lodge village sites, and for centuries of activity by native cultures. There is parking at each of the three main sites, and hiking trails link them. At the north end of the site (Big Hidatsa) there is a nature trail suitable for hiking and cross-country skiing. A bird checklist with species, season, and nesting information is available from the visitor center at the south end of the site. The busiest time is the tourist season, June through August.

Directions: *From Stanton, take Mercer County Road 37 (at the west end of town) north .5 mile to the visitor center.*

Ownership: NPS (745-3309)
Size: 1,758 acres   **Closest Town:** Stanton

Wild turkeys are not native to North Dakota. Efforts to transplant wild birds into suitable habitat have spread wild turkeys around the state.
MICHAEL S. SAMPLE

43 CROSS RANCH

Description: Three sites—Cross Ranch State Park, Cross Ranch Nature Preserve, and Smith Grove—that combine open cottonwood-dominated mixed forest, expanses of native mixed-grass prairie, and upland woody draws. Nearly 100 species of birds have been documented here including turkeys, great horned owls, red-tailed hawks, kestrels, and a huge variety of nesting songbirds. It is common to see deer and turkeys. Plovers and terns nest on sandbars in the Missouri River. Bison have been reintroduced on the preserve.

Viewing Information: There are more than sixteen miles of trails to hike in these sites, with viewing opportunities from the trails, from observation blinds, and from overlooks. To see plovers and terns nesting on the Missouri sandbars you need binoculars or a good spotting scope. A good bird guide will help identify other birds in the area. Deer are most easily seen in winter when the animals "yard up" during cold weather. Check at the visitor center in the park for interpretive brochures and events. Ask at preserve headquarters across the railroad tracks for the location of the bison or to arrange tours of the preserve. Please keep in mind that bison are wild animals, and that visitors are not allowed inside the bison enclosure. There is a fee for use of camping and other facilities at the park.

Directions: *To get to Cross Ranch State Park and Cross Ranch Nature Preserve from Mandan, go north on Collins Avenue to North Dakota 1806; go north on North Dakota 1806 twenty-nine miles to the site. From Washburn, go four miles west on North Dakota Highway 200A to Hensler, then six miles southeast on the gravel road. From Center, go east on North Dakota 25 ten miles to the Hensler turn, then north five miles and east three miles to the site. To get to Smith Grove, go four miles south from the Cross Ranch headquarters.*

Ownership: Cross Ranch State Park, NDPT (794-3731); Cross Ranch Nature Preserve; The Nature Conservancy (794-8741); Smith Grove Wildlife Management Area, NDGF (224-3344)
Size: 6,500 acres
Closest Town: Washburn

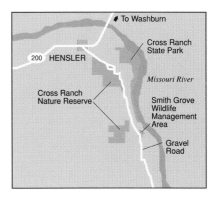

Description: A thirty-mile drive along the Missouri River north of Bismarck. The tour takes you through native river bottom woodlands, rolling native prairie interspersed with woody draws and buttes with rocky outcroppings, and river bottom wetlands. Wildlife to look for are waterfowl, especially giant Canada geese; least terns and piping plovers; bald eagles; upland birds such as turkeys and pheasants; white-tailed deer; and a wide variety of songbirds.

Viewing Information: The auto tour winds along the Missouri River, with designated stops at Double Ditch Historic Site, Steckel Boat Landing, and Painted Woods Wildlife Management Area. Waterfowl can be seen year-round all along the route, as can white-tailed deer, turkeys, and pheasants. Least terns and piping plovers can be seen during summer on sandbars in the river. Viewing bald eagles is most reliable spring and fall. Double Ditch offers a very scenic overlook of the Missouri, and was once the site of two Native American villages. Painted Woods WMA offers hiking through cottonwood-dominated hardwood forest along the river bottom and a spectacular river bottom wetland.

Directions: *From Interstate 94 in Bismarck, take the Divide exit and go north to the intersection with Burnt Boat Drive and turn west. Follow Burnt Boat Drive to the River Road. Turn north on the River Road to the junction with North Dakota 1804 at Pioneer Park to begin the tour north along the river. To take the tour from north to south, start at the junction of U.S. 83 and North Dakota 1804, about five miles south of Washburn.*

Ownership: PVT, NDGF (224-3344), NDPT (224-2525)
Size: Sixty-mile circuit **Closest Town:** Bismarck

The Missouri River between Bismarck and Garrison Dam is the last undammed stretch of this river in the state. Dam construction on the river has controlled the flooding which once created mudflats and sandbars necessary to regenerate the cottonwood forest. The decline in young cottonwood forest will inevitably lead to a decline in animal and plant diversity along the river.
KEITH KRAMER

45 FORT ABRAHAM LINCOLN STATE PARK

Description: Cottonwood-dominated river bottom forest and upland grassland associated with the Missouri River, and popular historic site and recreation area. View upland birds and songbirds, also small mammals such as cottontail rabbits, ground squirrels, skunks, and raccoons. White-tailed deer and geese are also common. Wildflowers bloom in spring and early summer.

Viewing Information: A .75-mile interpretive trail winds you through many of the park's habitats. Pick up the brochure available at the trailhead, and bring your binoculars for the treetops and overlooks of the river. A good place to view deer and Canada geese in the fall and early winter is the overlook of the Missouri obtained by looking east from the park entrance north of the road to the visitor's center. This overlook is also good for viewing hawks in the fall and spring. The site of the reconstructed blockhouses is often good for viewing deer on fall evenings. There is a fee for camping and day use at the park.

Directions: From Mandan, go south on North Dakota 1806 four miles to the entrance to the park.

Ownership: NDPT (663-9571)
Size: 1,006 acres   **Closest Town:** Mandan

46 OAHE WILDLIFE MANAGEMENT AREA

Description: Missouri River hardwood forest with oxbow wetlands interspersed with grass uplands, and croplands managed as wildlife food plots. The WMA is on both sides of the river. Two water-control projects have improved habitat for nesting waterfowl. View giant Canada geese, piping plover, great blue herons, American bittern, pheasants, sharp-tailed grouse, many species of songbirds, and white-tailed deer.

Viewing Information: The site straddles the river and can be reached by land or water. Roads and trails can be rutted and muddy in spring and in wet weather, and trails can be blocked by trees or low-hanging branches. But the chances for viewing giant Canada geese spring through fall are excellent. Wood ducks are found here spring and fall. Great blue herons and American bittern are seen spring and summer, and white-tailed deer and upland birds are year-round residents. Hiking is allowed anywhere on the WMA, as is primitive camping.

Directions: From Bismarck, go south on North Dakota 1804 four miles. From Mandan, go south on North Dakota 1806 ten miles.

Ownership: COE, managed by NDGF (224-3344)
Size: 23,500 acres   **Closest Town:** Bismarck, Mandan

47 | MORTON COUNTY WILDLIFE MANAGEMENT AREA

Description: A sharp-tailed grouse lek or dancing ground in a section of mixed-grass prairie.

Viewing Information: The North Dakota Game and Fish Department places a three-person observation blind next to the dancing ground in early April each year. The blind is open to the public, but you must make reservations with the Bismarck office of the Game and Fish Department. Be very quiet approaching the blind. The birds will be on the ground before sunrise, and may leave as you approach. Enter the blind, get settled, and the birds should return shortly. The earlier you arrive, the more likely the grouse are to return to the lek. Note: the trail leading into the WMA is unimproved, and in wet weather might be impassable. If you can, go to the site the day before to familiarize yourself with the area.

Directions: From the Heart River bridge in Mandan, go south on North Dakota 6 approximately 10.7 miles to the trail leading east to the WMA. Follow the trail east up the hill and along the north boundary fence of the WMA. After about .75 mile you'll see a wooden sign pointing in the direction of the blind. Enter through the turnstile, and walk from there. On foot, follow the boundary fence to another sign near the top of a ridge to the east. Follow the ridge southeast to another sign. The blind is located on this ridge. There is also an old trail along the top of the ridge that passes near the lek. You may be able to follow this trail with a flashlight.

Ownership: NDGF (221-6343 or 221-6314)
Size: 640 acres   **Closest Town:** St. Anthony

The site of Fort Abraham Lincoln has attracted people as well as wildlife. Prior to the fort, this was the site of a Mandan Indian village in the mid-1600s. KEITH KRAMER   61

48 HEART BUTTE WILDLIFE MANAGEMENT AREA

Description: An area along the western end of Lake Tschida and the Heart River channel managed for wildlife. Habitats within the WMA are willow river bottoms, hardwood draws, steep, eroded river breaks, and planted shelter belts. Typical wildlife species are white-tailed and mule deer, upland birds such as sharp-tailed grouse and pheasants, and nesting ducks in the river channel west of the reservoir. Canada geese appear during migration periods, and cliff swallows nest in the steep hillsides. Rattlesnakes may also be encountered.

Viewing Information: View ducks along the channel at the west end during spring and summer. White-tailed deer and mule deer are in the shelter belts—look for mule deer in the cedar plantings at dusk and dawn. There are two main access points to this part of the WMA (see the directions below), but access within the WMA is on foot. Roads to the site are gravel and dirt and during wet and snowy weather may be impassable.

Directions: *From Glen Ullin, go south on North Dakota 49 to Heart Butte Dam, about eighteen miles. Circle around the reservoir to the south and take the first gravel road west. Go either six or nine miles to roads that go north to the WMA.*

Ownership: BOR, managed by NDGF (224-3344)
Size: 5,500 acres
Closest Town: Elgin

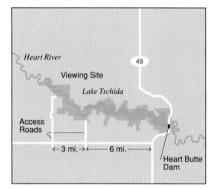

Watching the courtship dance of male sharp-tailed grouse is popular in North Dakota. Observation blinds can be reserved at Morton County WMA, the Audubon Society's Alkali Lake Sanctuary and many of the larger national wildlife refuges.
HARRY ENGLES

Description: An impoundment on the Heart River. The western two-thirds of the site is managed as wildlife habitat. The area features heavy riparian habitat along the meandering Heart River channel, with some marshy and brushy habitat adjacent to it. An area of cottonwood snags, killed when the lake was filled, provides an unusual opportunity to view nesting great blue herons. Other species to look for are Canada geese, white pelicans, ducks, and pheasants.

Viewing Information: The site is most reliable for wading birds such as great blue herons and double-crested cormorants in spring and summer, peaking in late April to early July. In spring the site is also excellent for mallards and green-winged teal. Yellow-headed blackbirds and marsh wrens are common. A colony of pelicans nests at the site, and there are Canada geese each spring. The heron rookery is accessible by boat, but bring binoculars so you don't disturb the birds. The site is also a popular recreation area for the city of Dickinson. A brochure explaining rules and fees is available at the main entrance.

Directions: *Take the westernmost Dickinson exit from I 94 and go south one mile to the intersection with Villard Street West (old Highway 10). Take Villard Street 1.6 miles west to 50th Avenue SW. Turn south and go .6 mile to the main entrance. Or, instead of turning south on 50th, proceed either one or two miles farther on Villard to roads which go south to the wildlife area of the site.*

Ownership: BOR, managed by Dickinson Parks and Recreation (225-2074)
Size: 2,260 acres   **Closest Town:** Dickinson

Prime nesting habitat for great blue herons are stands of large dead trees. Such areas were once created by floods, but are now more often created by rising waters in reservoirs. Heron rookeries may be viewed at Patterson Lake and Oahe WMA.
SHERM SPOELSTRA

50 BOWMAN-HALEY DAM

Description: Impoundment on the North Fork of the Grand River. The site features level grassland surrounding the lake, with a shelterbelt system of Siberian elm, green ash, Russian olive, and evergreens. Canada geese are found here, also dabbling ducks such as mallards, pintails, gadwalls, and blue-winged teal. Other wildlife includes ring-necked pheasant, sharp-tailed grouse, gray partridge, white-tailed deer, and the occasional mule deer.

Viewing Information: The best times for viewing waterfowl are during spring and fall migrations. Canada geese begin to move into the site as the ice breaks up in April, and remain through May. The build-up begins again in late September and continues through October. Pheasants are in the area year-round as are white-tailed deer. Nearby food plots bring in mule deer; the best time for viewing is in fall, before hunting season. There is good viewing of waterfowl from the picnic area.

Directions: *From Bowman, go south on U.S. 85 for eleven miles. Turn east on the gravel road and go eight miles. Turn south and travel two miles to the site.*

Ownership: COE (572-6494)
Size: 6,720 acres   **Closest Town:** Bowman

51 BIG GUMBO

Description: Arid mixed-grass prairie, with scattered sagebrush, patches of buffalo grass, and scattered Rocky Mountain juniper on the ridge tops. The most typical wildlife species here are sage grouse and pronghorn antelope. Watch for golden eagles and ferruginous hawks, and upland species such as the chestnut-collared longspur, lark bunting, and Brewer's sparrow. You may also encounter bull snakes and prairie rattlesnakes.

Viewing Information: The best season to come to Big Gumbo for viewing wildlife is in the spring, especially a wet spring. Then it is among the best sites in the state for roadside viewing of pronghorn antelope, sage grouse, and chestnut-collared longspur. Eagles and hawks can be seen overhead, and other birds both seen and heard across the landscape. A good bird guide is useful. Big Gumbo is a large area, and side roads through it are not very good. In wet weather—as likely in spring—they can be impassable. Under any but the best conditions, stay on the well-graveled West River Road.

Directions: *From Marmarth, .25 mile west on U.S. 12, then turn south on the West River (Camp Crook) Road. Go eighteen miles south to Big Gumbo.*

Ownership: BLM (225-9148)
Size: 20,000 acres   **Closest Town:** Marmarth

Description: An area of steep-sided scoria bluffs and the only place in North Dakota where limber pines grow. The origin of these trees is unknown—they are far from the mountains where they are typically found. The setting here is rugged and picturesque, overlooking the Little Missouri River and Cannonball Creek. The area provides habitat for mule deer, sage grouse, red-tailed hawks, and golden eagles. You may see poorwills, chickadees, mountain bluebirds, rufous-sided towhees, lazuli buntings, and Clark's nutcracker, a bird that feeds on the seeds of limber pines. There are rattlesnakes.

Viewing Information: Limber Pines is for those with a sense of adventure and a four-wheel-drive vehicle. The directions that follow should be used together with a U.S. Forest Service map of the Little Missouri National Grassland and only in dry weather. Limber Pines is recommended as a spring and early fall site—it is hot country in July and August. September is colorful with blazing star and goldenrod. There are no facilities at the site, so bring plenty of drinking water.

Directions: From U.S. 12 just west of Marmarth, take the gravel road north for approximately fourteen miles (you must ford a creek a few miles north of Marmarth) to a jeep trail near the crossing of Cannonball Creek. The turn onto the jeep trail is sharp and easy to miss. If you reach a second ford on the gravel road, you have missed the jeep trail. Follow the jeep trail east along the ridge on the south side of Cannonball Creek for about five miles to the site. There are gates along the jeep trail. Respect private landowners along the trail, and close the gates behind you.

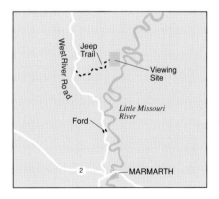

Ownership: USFS: 225-5151
Size: 200 acres
Closest Town: Marmarth

53 BURNING COAL VEIN

Description: An area of badlands along the Little Missouri River and Sand Creek, with the only major stand of ponderosa pine in North Dakota. Site takes its name from an underground coal vein which burned slowly for more than a hundred years. The area is fine habitat and a good viewing opportunity for mule deer and wild turkeys year-round. There is good viewing and listening for rufous-sided towhee, chickadees, nuthatches, and poorwills. June through August, it is possible to see Audubon's warbler—the only place in the state where they nest. Wildflowers bloom early in summer on the scoria and sandstone knolls. Also hiding in the scoria are tiny scorpions, which are not a danger to people.

Viewing Information: The site offers an excellent early morning/late evening roadside viewing opportunity for deer, turkeys, and porcupines along the gravel road winding through this rough topography. The Forest Service operates a non-fee campground at the Burning Coal Vein site, with an overlook of the area and a foot trail among the sandstone outcrops. When you are walking, beware of rattlesnakes. Bring enough drinking water— there is no source of drinking water at the campground.

Directions: *From U.S. 85 two miles west of Amidon, (where U.S. 85 turns south) go one mile west on the gravel road. Turn north and follow signs to Burning Coal Vein campground, approximately twelve miles.*

Ownership: USFS (225-5151)
Size: 200 acres   **Closest Town:** Amidon

Although a native species, pronghorn antelope have been hit hard by severe winters in North Dakota. Biologists theorize that manmade changes such as fences prevent the animals from moving to areas with better food and cover, making them vulnerable to the weather. DAPHNE KINZLER

Description: More than a million acres of diverse prairie and badlands habitats. The area is home to several hundred wildlife species. Some of particular interest are mule deer, white-tailed deer, bighorn sheep, prairie dogs, pronghorn antelope, wild turkeys, sharp-tailed grouse, and golden eagles.

Viewing Information: Given the diversity of habitats and species it would be to your advantage to go to the district U.S. Forest Service ranger stations in Dickinson and Watford City for assistance in finding viewing opportunities for your particular interests. Maps of the grassland are also available at the ranger stations. For additional viewing opportunities in the Little Missouri National Grassland, refer to sites 53 and 55 of this guide.

Directions: The McKenzie Ranger District office is located on the west side of U.S. 85, one mile south of Watford City. To reach the Medora Ranger District office, take North Dakota 22 (Dickinson-Killdeer) exit from I 94. Go north on North Dakota 22 to 161 West 21st Street, Dickinson.

Ownership: USFS (842-2393, Watford City; 225-5151, Dickinson)
Size: 1.2 million acres   **Closest Town:** Watford City or Dickinson

55 **LITTLE MISSOURI NATIONAL GRASSLAND AUTO TOUR**

Description: A self-guided automobile tour of the southern portion of the Little Missouri National Grassland. View mule deer, bighorn sheep, sharp-tailed grouse, pronghorn antelope, golden eagles, and prairie dogs, among many other species.

Viewing Information: Tour begins and ends at the Medora Visitor Center of the South Unit of Theodore Roosevelt National Park. A guide brochure with animal and plant checklists is available at the visitor center. The tour is approximately fifty-eight miles long. Watch out for poison ivy in shaded woody areas and for rattlesnakes. When parking, get as far off the highway as possible. Bad weather can make these roads difficult to travel. There are no restrooms along the tour route.

Directions: From Interstate 94 at Medora, go to the Medora Visitor Center of the South Unit of Theodore Roosevelt National Park. This visitor center is at the west end of the town of Medora.

Ownership: USFS (225-5151)
Size: Fifty-eight mile tour   **Closest Town:** Medora

BADLANDS

North Dakota's badlands are a maze of steep-sided draws and ridges formed over thousands of years as the Little Missouri River carved the land surface to depths of up to five hundred feet. South-facing badlands slopes are barren but for sage, cactus, and yucca; in the draws, where moisture collects and the sun is less punishing, chokecherry bushes and green ash can flourish. North slopes, with little or no direct sunlight, are often covered with Rocky Mountain juniper. Here, where the terrain and the vegetation can vary markedly within a short distance, mule deer can satisfy all their needs.

Mule deer fawns in North Dakota are usually born in June. During their first weeks of life, fawns are extremely vulnerable to predators such as coyotes. The badlands, with brushy hiding places in a maze of washes and draws, greatly increase a fawn's chances for survival.

The ash stands, brushy washes, and juniper provide for other needs as well. During the summer and fall, mule deer feed on the season's new growth. The washes provide shade on hot days, a source of water, and escape routes from danger. During cold winter nights, deer tend to move up the sides of buttes into warmer air in the sheltered stands of juniper. Because cold air settles, temperatures in the bottom of washes can be as much as seventeen degrees colder than in the juniper stands fifty feet

A woody draw in the badlands, prime mule deer habitat.
KEITH KRAMER

above. The junipers also block falling snow, reducing snow depths within the stands.

If all has gone well for a mule deer doe during the winter, the early flush of green grasses and forbs on the butte tops in April provide much-needed nutrition for her and for the fawn she carries in her womb. In June, the badlands will again provide cover and food for new fawns, and the cycle of the seasons will repeat. Mule deer in the badlands have adapted to these conditions just as ducks have adapted their breeding behavior to the cycles of prairie potholes. Though the environments are very different, the implications for conservationists are much the same. The relationship between an animal and its habitat is complex; and therein lies its strength. Conservation must be directed at conserving habitats in all their complexity, in all their diversity. Only then can it be effective.

You can tell mule deer bucks from whitetail bucks by their antlers. Whitetail antlers have a single beam on each side of the head with unbranched tines projecting from it; mule deer antlers branch.
C. D. GRONDAHL

56 THEODORE ROOSEVELT NATIONAL PARK—SOUTH UNIT

Description: The South Unit is among the most diverse and easily accessible wildlife viewing sites in North Dakota. The park contains many habitats, including river bottom along the Little Missouri, badland slopes, and prairie grasslands. Buttes, tablelands, and valleys vary from the sparse vegetation of south-facing slopes to dense juniper stands on north-facing slopes. There is premier viewing of bison, mule deer, wild horses, prairie dogs, and—if you are fortunate—elk. Other species include golden eagles, coyote, magpies, burrowing owls, horned toads, badgers, porcupines, various species of songbirds, and rattlesnakes. Wildflowers bloom throughout the growing season, including sego lily, prince's plume, leopard lily, bluebells, cacti, evening star, and yucca.

Viewing Information: Viewing opportunities are too diverse to list. Among them are hiking and backcountry trails, an auto tour loop, and guided nature walks. The park is a year-round opportunity. Stop at the Medora Visitor Center for guides to park activities, trail maps, wildlife checklists, and other information about the natural and human history of the park. Watch out for bison on the road—they are wild. When walking, be alert for snakes. Don't try to feed the animals. The busiest time is the tourist season, June through August.

Directions: *From Interstate 94 near Medora, take the Medora exit to the Medora Visitor Center, or take the Painted Canyon exit to the Painted Canyon Visitor Center and rest area.*

Ownership: NPS (623-4466)
Size: 46,128 acres   **Closest Town:** Medora

The badlands landscape of the South Unit of Theodore Roosevelt National Park was formed by rain, wind, and the Little Missouri River.
KEITH KRAMER

Description: A lake/wetland complex surrounded by native prairie and planted trees. The site is an oasis for waterfowl and shorebirds in this semiarid region. Look for Canada geese, snow geese, and white-fronted geese; twenty species of ducks; a variety of shorebirds including piping plover; ring-necked pheasants, sharp-tailed grouse, and gray partridge and bald eagles.

Viewing Information: This is the only site for some miles to see waterfowl in large numbers. Canada geese nest here, and are seen spring through fall. Snow and white-fronted geese stop over during spring and fall migrations, March through April and late September/early October. Piping plover nest on the refuge—talk to the refuge manager about them. Many ducks nest here, and can be viewed spring through summer. The uplands provide year-round habitat for pheasants and other upland birds, and the wooded areas provide food and cover for white-tailed deer. Gravel roads circle most of the refuge, allowing viewing from a vehicle. Binoculars or a spotting scope are a must. Walking access is restricted in places on the refuge—watch for signs. Stop at the refuge headquarters or a kiosk at the entrance to the picnic area for maps and brochures.

Directions: *From the junction of North Dakota 200 and North Dakota 22 near Killdeer, go 5.5 miles east, and turn south to the refuge headquarters.*

Ownership: USFWS (548-8110)
Size: 3,200 acres   **Closest Town:** Dunn Center

Bison were reintroduced to the South Unit of Theodore Roosevelt National Park in 1956 when 29 animals were moved from Fort Niobrara National Wildlife Refuge in Nebraska. The North Unit herd was started in 1962. HAROLD UMBER   71

58 KILLDEER MOUNTAINS LOOP TOUR

Description: A scenic drive around a range of hills with flat-topped plateaus and extensive erosion-shaped spurs. The Killdeer Mountains harbor the largest upland forest in the southwest corner of the state, and are a biological crossroads for native plants and animals. An adjacent wildlife management area gives way to grassland, and badlands on the west end. Species to look for are mule deer and elk, especially at dusk and dawn; coyotes in the early morning; golden eagles, turkey vultures, and hawks overhead; beaver in their ponds along the pass; turkeys and a small introduced population of ruffed grouse in the adjacent WMA; and a wildflower show all summer long.

Viewing Information: The Killdeer Mountains are privately owned, so this is essentially a driving tour. There are places where it's possible to pull over to the side of the road, but if you get out of your car for a better look, please respect the fences. Also try to get as far off the traveled part of the road as possible. Hiking is allowed in the wildlife management area to the west of the Killdeer Mountains.

Directions: *From the junction of North Dakota 22 and North Dakota 200 just south of the town of Killdeer, go north on North Dakota 22 through Killdeer about 9.8 miles. Turn west on the gravel road. After 3.3 miles, the gravel road forks; take the left-hand fork, and continue 2.6 miles. The road forks again here; take the right-hand fork. Continue until the "T" (another 1.3 miles), and turn south. Continue south 8.6 miles, then east one mile, and south one mile to North Dakota 200 (at the Killdeer Battlefield sign). Turn east and return to your starting point (nine miles).*

Ownership: Tour, state and county roads; Wildlife Management Area, NDGF (227-2343)
Size: Tour, 36.6 miles; WMA, 7,051 acres   **Closest Town:** Killdeer

The Killdeer Mountains area has North Dakota's greatest diversity of big game animals. The area is home to bighorn sheep, elk, pronghorn, mule deer, and white-tailed deer.
CRAIG BIHRLE

59 LITTLE MISSOURI STATE PARK

Description: Badlands terrain with buttes, ravines, plateaus, and crevices carved by erosion. Sage, yucca, and cactus flourish on south-facing slopes. In more protected places with moisture, there are grasses and brush. Woodlands thrive on north slopes. Area is prime habitat for mule deer, coyote, bobcat, and birds including golden and bald eagles, cedar waxwing, and prairie falcon.

Viewing Information: Site is best explored on horseback, with more than seventy-five miles of trails. There is a horse corral, horse rental concessions, and guide service on the site. But it is a tremendous opportunity for hikers as well. Chances of seeing mule deer in the park are excellent year-round; bobcat and coyote live in the area, but are elusive. Binoculars and cameras are a must.

Directions: From Killdeer, go north on North Dakota 22 sixteen miles. Turn east on the gravel road, and go three miles to the site.

Ownership: NDPT (764-8901)
Size: 5,900 acres   **Closest Town:** Killdeer

60 THEODORE ROOSEVELT NATIONAL PARK—NORTH UNIT

Description: The North Unit of North Dakota's only national park. Like the South Unit, the park contains diverse habitats, including river bottom, grassy plains, and badlands cut with ravines and breaks. Bison, white-tailed deer, mule deer, and prairie dogs are seen here, also longhorn steers. The park has a list of 179 species of birds that have been identified, including many hawks, golden eagles, sharp-tailed grouse, great blue herons, and many songbirds.

Viewing Information: Many opportunities for viewing wildlife. There is an auto tour, and trails (some are self-guided nature trails) of varying lengths and difficulties. Backcountry hiking and camping are also permitted. Bison, longhorn steers, and prairie dogs are relatively easy to watch—the usual warnings about wild animals apply to all of these. For songbirds and wildflowers, come in spring and early summer—many birds nest here, and are present through the fall. Golden eagles and great horned owls are fairly common, even in winter. Stop at the visitor center to pick up brochures and wildlife checklists.

Directions: From Watford City, go south on U.S. 85 for fifteen miles to the park entrance.

Ownership: NPS (842-2337 or 623-4466)
Size: 24,070 acres   **Closest Town:** Watford City

61 FORT BUFORD STATE HISTORIC SITE

Description: The confluence of two major rivers, and the intersection of major migration corridors for waterfowl and wading birds. The largely undeveloped confluence of the Yellowstone and Missouri gives a glimpse of the site as Lewis and Clark may have seen it nearly 200 years ago. Species to look for are geese, ducks, sandhill cranes, cormorants, gulls, white pelicans, and western grebes on the river; white-tailed deer, badgers, beavers, and muskrats in wooded and marshy areas; and owls, hawks, and eagles. The site offers an opportunity to view paddlefish, a prehistoric fish four to five feet long and forty-five to 100 pounds. This is the only area in North Dakota where the fish can legally be caught.

Viewing Information: The confluence is active in the spring and early summer with ducks, cormorants, gulls, white pelicans, and western grebes. The fall migration brings geese and, in some years, good numbers of sandhill cranes. The riparian habitat along the river—large cottonwoods with red and diamond willow and some second growth where it has been burned—provides forage for white-tailed deer. Views of the confluence are good from the picnic area and from the river itself. Golden eagles and owls can often be seen overhead and in the tall cottonwoods, and bald eagles arrive in the winter after freeze-up. There is a path that goes down to the river bottom from the picnic area through the different habitats below. This path encounters a private fence—please respect it. The path is best taken in the fall because of swampy conditions in spring and large numbers of mosquitoes in summer. Paddlefish can be viewed at the boat ramp in May as fishermen bring them in.

Directions: From Williston, take U.S. 2 west to the junction with North Dakota 1804. Turn south on North Dakota 1804 and follow the road along the river (approximately thirteen miles) to the Fort Buford site turnoff.

Ownership: SHSND (572-9034)
Size: 180 acres   **Closest Town:** Williston

Turkey vultures locate carrion with their acute sense of smell, and may be seen soaring along the Missouri River breaks.

Description: A cattail marsh fed by seepage from the Missouri River through a levee system and discharge from water treatment ponds from the town of Williston. Wildlife to look for includes ducks, particularly blue-winged teal and gadwalls, canvasbacks, and wood ducks; Canada geese; raptors, particularly great horned owls, goshawks, and bald and golden eagles; and eared grebes. There is a large pheasant population at the site and abundant white-tailed deer.

Viewing Information: Access is limited to walking the roads on top and below the levee. Walking the road on top of the levee gives a good view of wildlife activity both in the marsh and on the Missouri River. The road below runs four miles along the edge of the marsh. The best viewing for geese and ducks begins when the ice goes out in early spring, although there are Canada geese through the summer. Best time for raptors is late fall and early winter, especially for golden and bald eagles— viewing is quite good from the upper road. Feeders just off the lower road attract white-tailed deer and pheasants. Walking the lower road is best in fall when mosquitoes have died off.

Directions: *In Williston, at the junction of North Dakota 1804 and East Dakota Parkway, turn south and go .75 mile (across the railroad tracks) to the parking lot.*

Ownership: COE (572-6494)
Size: 800 acres   **Closest Town:** Williston

Williston Marsh features a large population of ring-necked pheasants. Feeders at the site are good places to look for these birds. LARRY R. DITTO

63 LEWIS AND CLARK STATE PARK

Description: A state park on one of the upper bays of Lake Sakakawea. The park contains a segment of the Missouri River breaks with native and introduced grasses, small areas of woody draws, and badlands outcrops. Wildlife to look for are common native upland birds, exotics such as ring-neck pheasants, cottontail rabbits, and common native prairie plants.

Viewing Information: This park has the largest area of native prairie in the state park system, and the best wildlife viewing is on foot. The park is a popular recreation area in the summer; viewing wildlife is best in early to late spring, when the wildflowers come into bloom and the western meadowlark announces the arrival of the season.

Directions: From Williston, go east on North Dakota 1804 sixteen miles to the junction with Williams County Road 15. Turn south on County Road 15 and go three miles to the park.

Ownership: NDPT (859-3071)
Size: 490 acres   **Closest Town:** Williston

64 ALKALI LAKE

Description: An alkali wetland complex, with alkali wetland basins, freshwater basins, springs, and gently rolling native prairie. The site is part of the Bureau of Land Management's Watchable Wildlife Program. Species to look for are Canada geese, mallards, green-winged teal, upland sandpiper, American avocet, marbled godwit, Wilson's phalarope, Baird's sparrow, and other waterfowl associated with alkaline wetlands. It is also possible to view nesting piping plovers here, a threatened species.

Viewing Information: The best time to visit Alkali Lake is in the spring when birds such as American avocet and piping plover are breeding, beginning early to mid-May. Look for birds on sparsely vegetated shorelines or mud flats. DO NOT DISTURB THE BIRDS—keep your distance and use optical equipment. Much of the land around Alkali Lake is privately owned—keep to the land managed by BLM (it's clearly marked)—or view from county roads.

Directions: From Williston, go thirty-one miles north on U.S. 85 to the junction with North Dakota 50. Turn east on North Dakota 50 and go one mile to Williams County Road 9. Turn north on County Road 9 for .4 mile to Alkali Lake.

Ownership: BLM (225-9148)
Size: 320 acres   **Closest Town:** Appam

Description: A large site with rolling northern mixed-grass prairie, dotted with a wide spectrum of wetlands and lakes—the prairie pothole region as it might have been before settlement. Lostwood has high breeding populations of mallards, gadwalls, blue-winged teal, giant Canada geese, and shorebirds such as avocets and upland sandpipers. Bird watchers visit here for the abundant grasshopper sparrow, Baird's sparrow, and Sprague's pipit. Raptors include red-tailed and Swainson's hawks, and short-eared, long-eared, and great horned owls. Sharp-tailed grouse are common.

Viewing Information: There are many ways to view wildlife at Lostwood. It offers year-round opportunities, with an auto tour and hiking trails in the spring, summer, and fall, and snowshoeing and cross-country skiing in winter. In spring, an observation blind is set up at a sharp-tailed grouse dancing ground. In fall and early winter, when waterfowl concentrations are high, look for golden and bald eagles. Prairie falcons and gyrfalcons are winter visitors. Stop at the refuge headquarters for brochures, pamphlets, a guide to the auto tour, and a wildlife checklist. Refuge office hours are 7:30 a.m. to 4:00 p.m. Monday through Friday. Prime viewing seasons are May to mid-July and late September through October.

Directions: *From Stanley, go twenty-one miles north on North Dakota 8 to the refuge entrance.*

Ownership: USFWS (848-2722)
Size: 26,900 acres   **Closest Town:** Kenmare

Marbled godwits depend on water, though they nest on grassland, sometimes a considerable distance from water. Best viewing of these birds is at Alkali Lake, Stump Lake, and Sullys Hill.
LYNN BENDER

66 DES LACS NATIONAL WILDLIFE REFUGE

Description: A twenty-six-mile lake and marsh area, bordered by prairie and wooded coulees. The refuge has good habitat diversity, and is along a migration corridor for birds. During the peak of migration, waterfowl populations on the refuge may exceed 200,000 birds. It is an excellent site for snow geese. In the spring, watch the courtship antics of western grebes, and view pied-billed, red-necked, horned, and eared grebes nesting on the refuge. Bird watchers should look for LeConte's sparrow.

Viewing Information: The best seasons for waterfowl are the annual spring and fall migrations. The peak month is October, and the best vantage point is the seven-mile "old lake road" south of Kenmare. The breeding season for western grebes begins in mid-May. An observation blind for watching the spring courtship ritual of sharp-tailed grouse is open (by reservation) April through June. Roads are unimproved. There are walking trails within the refuge. Brochures are available at the refuge headquarters and at a kiosk outside. A canoe launch site is located six miles north of the headquarters on the west side of the lake. Headquarters hours are 7:30 a.m. to 4:00 p.m. weekdays.

Directions: *From Kenmare, go .5 mile west on Ward County Road 2 to the refuge headquarters.*

Ownership: USFWS (385-4046)
Size: 19,544 acres   **Closest Town:** Kenmare

Western grebes are often watched during courtship as they sprint across the surface of the water. Some of the best places to view them are on the large refuges like Des Lacs.
LYNN BENDER

REGION FOUR:
LAKES AND GARDENS

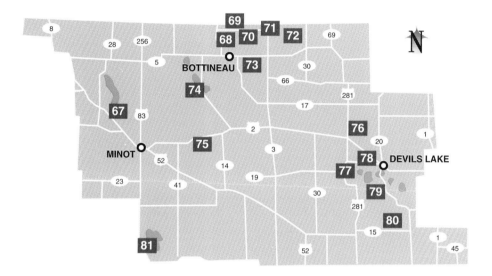

67 UPPER SOURIS NATIONAL WILDLIFE REFUGE

Description: A series of impoundments, marshes, and grasslands along the Souris River. The area attracts up to 100,000 birds during the spring and fall waterfowl migrations, and resident wildlife is diverse. In March and April, look for ducks and Canada geese; in October, look for snow geese. Five species of grebes nest on the refuge and can be viewed all summer. Birders will be able to find Baird's, LeConte's, and sharp-tailed sparrows and Sprague's pipit. White-tailed deer are common, as are sharp-tailed grouse. Lake Darling, a popular fishing lake, has northern pike, walleye, yellow perch, and smallmouth bass.

Viewing Information: A 3.5-mile scenic auto tour offers good viewing from your car. Mowed hiking trails double as cross- country ski trails in winter (they are not groomed). Canoe trails diversify viewing opportunities. During April and May, there is an observation blind to watch the courtship ritual of sharp-tailed grouse. Hunting and fishing are allowed on certain portions of the refuge. Brochures covering these activities and restrictions to other activities during hunting seasons are available at the headquarters. The headquarters is open 8:00 a.m. to 4:30 p.m. weekdays, and the refuge is open 5:00 a.m. to 10:00 p.m. daily. Stop at the refuge headquarters for wildlife checklists and other information about wildlife and management of the refuge.

Directions: *From Minot, go north on U.S. 83 thirteen miles. Turn west on Ward County Road 6 and go west twelve miles to the refuge headquarters.*

Ownership: USFWS (468-5467)
Size: 32,000 acres   **Closest Town:** Foxholm

Upper Souris NWR was established in 1935, when drought caused national concern for the duck population. Since the 1960s, the refuge has been increasingly important as a stopover for snow geese during the fall migration.
WILLIAM K. VINJE

68 STRAWBERRY LAKE

Description: A forty-acre lake and campground with a trailhead for many trails through the 6,000-acre Turtle Mountain State Forest. The forest is dominated by oak and aspen—good habitat for deer, moose, and ruffed grouse. Waterfowl are at the site spring, summer, and fall, peaking during the early spring and fall migration periods. There are songbirds all summer.

Viewing Information: There are miles of trails through the state forest; use Strawberry Lake as your starting point. A half-mile west of the campgrounds is a viewing tower. A boat ramp provides access to the lake. Best times for viewing are early morning and late evening. The site is excellent for deer and waterfowl spring and fall. Ruffed grouse can be heard drumming during the breeding season in spring, but the birds are hard to see. There are moose in the area as well, but you should count yourself fortunate if you see one.

Directions: *From the junction of North Dakota 14 and North Dakota 43 (north of Bottineau), go 1.5 miles east on North Dakota 43.*

Ownership: NDFS (228-3700)
Size: Forty acres   **Closest Town:** Bottineau

Blue-winged teal are one of the most common dabbling ducks of the prairie pothole region, along with mallards, pintails, and gadwalls. North Dakota's refuges and waterfowl production areas produce large numbers of ducks during the nesting season. SCOTT NIELSEN

81

ASPEN FOREST

North Dakota's aspen forests are concentrated in the Turtle Mountains and the Pembina Hills. The forests provide a home to many kinds of wildlife, but they are particularly important to ruffed grouse. Ruffed grouse need aspen to reach high population levels; but the simple presence of aspen trees will not guarantee good numbers of birds. To provide good year-round ruffed grouse habitat, the forest must have both young and old aspen trees and a thick shrub understory.

Aspen forests ten to twenty years old provide the best ruffed grouse breeding habitat. In spring, male grouse stand on fallen logs and "drum" out a mating call. They select logs that are above the forest floor and surrounded by thick brush. Here they can see potential mates, and can watch for predators approaching from the ground or air.

Twenty to thirty year-old forest provides ruffed grouse with nesting habitat. Nesting hens select sites with a relatively open forest floor. The nest is built at the base of a willow clump, up against a fallen log, or at the base of a tree so that the hen has an open view of approaching predators.

To grow and develop quickly, young grouse chicks need a high-protein diet of insects. Aspen forest one to ten years old provides abundant insect populations and a low, dense canopy of leaves to protect the chicks from owls and hawks. After about five weeks, the chicks are ready for a diet of leaves and the fruits

Aspen woods in North Dakota. BRUCE WENDT

of succulent plants, also found in this young forest.

In the fall, ruffed grouse move to the shelter and rich food source in the shrub understory of highbush cranberry, rose, nannyberry, and wolfberry. In winter, the birds eat the buds of beaked hazel, willow, and paper birch, and the buds of aspen trees, especially the buds of male trees twenty-five to forty years old.

Ruffed grouse are not the only birds that depend on different successional stages of trees in the aspen forest. Older forest regions benefit cavity-nesting birds such as woodpeckers, nuthatches, chickadees, and great-crested flycatchers. Middle-aged forests are home to magpies, kingbirds, and vireos. The dense undergrowth of new, young aspen attracts warblers and other secretive insect-eating birds. Aspen forest, like other habitats in North Dakota, is a complex system, and many different species have found a place in it. But natural fires—which once cleared areas of forest for regrowth—no longer occur. Forest managers have resorted to bulldozing areas of forest which are either too old or diseased in order to provide the different age classes of trees on which both ruffed grouse and nongame birds depend.

Ruffed grouse drumming on a log.
WILLIAM K. VINJE

69 LAKE METIGOSHE STATE PARK

Description: North Dakota's "north woods" state park, featuring woodland lakes, marshes, and oak-aspen forest. Typical animals of the area are deer, moose, and innumerable small mammals such as squirrels, woodchucks, raccoons, and snowshoe hares. Water birds such as osprey, herons, bitterns, and gulls are common. A fine site for beaver and muskrats—their houses are seen throughout the area. Lake Metigoshe offers perhaps the easiest access in the state for hearing ruffed grouse drum in the spring. The Turtle Mountains Environmental Learning Center (on-site) is open to groups by reservation. There is an unusual opportunity here to watch western painted turtles laying eggs in mid to late June, and the marshes host a variety of frogs.

Viewing Information: The park offers a variety of viewing opportunities. There is an extensive trail system for hiking, some of which is groomed for cross-country skiing in winter. The Old Oak Trail—a three-mile self-guided hiking trail—features an observation platform overlooking School Section Lake. A brochure is available at the trailhead. Roads through the park offer some opportunity to view from a vehicle, and there is a boat ramp. The site is a busy recreation area in the summer.

Directions: *From Bottineau, go north on North Dakota 14 to the junction with North Dakota 43. Go east on North Dakota 43 to the road leading to the park. Watch for signs.*

Ownership: NDPT (263-4651)
Size: 1,200 acres   **Closest Town:** Bottineau

The painted turtle, North Dakota's most common turtle, is one of the basking turtles, and can most often be seen sunbathing, two or more to a log, in North Dakota's slow-moving rivers and creeks.
C. D. GRONDAHL

70 PELICAN & SANDY LAKES

Description: An area of small lakes, marshes, and woodlands in the heart of the Turtle Mountains. Managed as a primitive area, the site features waterfowl when there is open water, songbirds spring through fall, and white-tailed deer year-round. Look for ducks such as mallards, pintails, and wood ducks; also herons, grebes, pelicans, and cormorants. The site offers a fairly good chance of seeing moose, especially in spring and fall.

Viewing Information: Viewing here is primarily on foot through an extensive trail system. Peak times are during spring and fall migrations of waterfowl and other birds. Watch for deer and moose during spring as new growth comes onto the trees and brush and during the fall mating season. Other birds and small mammals can be seen spring through fall. Wood ducks are at the site spring through summer, nesting in artificial nesting boxes. There is a boat ramp and a fee for camping.

Directions: *From Lake Metigoshe, go six miles east on North Dakota 43 and turn south on the gravel road to the site.*

Ownership: NDFS (228-3700)
Size: 1,400 acres   **Closest Town:** Bottineau

71 INTERNATIONAL PEACE GARDEN

Description: A formal and natural garden dedicated in 1932 to peace between Canada and the United States. The site is near the center of the continent, and spans the international boundary. It features several natural lakes, two impoundments—one on each side of the border—and swamps, marshes, and forest typical of the Turtle Mountains. Featured are water birds, including geese, ducks, herons, and gulls. White-tailed deer are common, as are muskrat, beaver, mink, and weasel. Fortunate visitors may see a moose.

Viewing Information: Much of the garden is managed as a "natural zone." The Canadian Natural Drive—a self-guided auto tour—offers wildlife viewing by car. There is a 1.5-mile hiking trail on the Canadian side and trails on the United States side which link various facilities, all offering viewing opportunities. Picnic sites take advantage of the natural features of the area. The best time to visit for wildlife viewing is the off-season, October through May. Facilities are open summers only.

Directions: *Go north on North Dakota 3 to the Canadian border.*

Ownership: International Peace Garden, Inc.
(263-4390)
Size: 2,339 acres   **Closest Town:** Dunseith

72 WAKOPA WILDLIFE MANAGEMENT AREA

Description: Aspen woods interspersed with lakes, wetlands, and grassland. For aspen woods to be ideal wildlife habitat, there must be stands of trees of varying ages. By bulldozing overage and understocked stands, Wakopa is maintained as good habitat for deer, moose, elk, snowshoe hare, and ruffed grouse. Other species on Wakopa WMA include foxes, coyotes, lynx, raccoons, skunks, weasels, mink, beaver, fox squirrels, muskrats, and woodchucks. Loons are summer residents.

Viewing Information: Wakopa is a year-round opportunity, with best viewing spring through fall. An auto tour takes you through part of the WMA. An east-west road splits the WMA into two units; the north unit is closed to vehicles. The entire WMA is open to walking access, and more than fifteen miles of walking trails are mowed each year. These make ideal cross-country ski trails in winter. Four boat ramps provide canoe access to the area. Opportunities to see deer and moose are also good in winter. Stays of longer than ten days require a permit from the Game and Fish Department.

Directions: *From the junction of U.S. 281 and North Dakota 43 north of Dunseith, go east 8.5 miles to the main entrance to Wakopa WMA.*

Ownership: NDGF (662-3617)
Size: 6,800 acres   **Closest Town:** St. John

Lake Stormon, on Canada's side of the International Peace Garden, is maintained
at a constant water level for nesting ducks. KEITH KRAMER

73   LORDS LAKE NATIONAL WILDLIFE REFUGE

Description: A shallow lake surrounded by agricultural land and some grassland. The site is a concentration area for migrating waterfowl, particularly snow geese, tundra swans, and ducks.

Viewing Information: The land surrounding Lords Lake NWR is privately owned. Viewing opportunities are limited to the county road. However, viewing from the road is excellent, especially during spring and fall, when large numbers of birds side-slip into the water from a few hundred feet above you. Pull well off the traveled part of the road.

Directions: *From Bottineau, go east on North Dakota 5 twelve miles. Turn south on the gravel road and go 1.5 miles to Lords Lake.*

Ownership: PVT, under easement to USFWS (768-2548)
Size: 1,915 acres   **Closest Town:** Dunseith

74   J. CLARK SALYER NATIONAL WILDLIFE REFUGE

Description: The largest wildlife refuge in North Dakota, featuring marshes, meadows, river bottom hardwood forest, and sandhill prairie at the south end. More than 250 species of birds have been recorded here; peak numbers of snow geese on the refuge approach 150,000, and total waterfowl numbers approach 250,000. View songbirds such as LeConte's, Baird's and sharp-tailed sparrows. Other birds include sharp-tailed grouse, white pelicans, eared grebes, and black-crowned night herons. Common mammals include white-tailed deer, mink, muskrats, red fox, and coyote.

Viewing Information: Near the headquarters are an observation tower and bird watching platforms. A twenty-two-mile auto tour is open year-round, but is not maintained in winter and can be treacherous after heavy rain. Check with the refuge headquarters for road conditions. There is another five-mile auto tour open spring through September. Thirteen miles of the Souris River have been designated part of the National Canoe Trails System. In April, the refuge operates an observation blind for sharp-tailed grouse, and a walking path through the sandhills passes near ruffed grouse drumming sites. Information, brochures, bird checklists, and maps are available at the self-service visitor station. The refuge is open 5:00 a.m. to 10:00 p.m. daily, and the refuge headquarters is open 8:00 a.m. to 4:30 p.m. weekdays.

Directions: *From Upham, go two miles north on North Dakota 14 to the refuge headquarters.*

Ownership: USFWS (768-2548)
Size: 58,700 acres   **Closest Town:** Upham

75 DENBIGH EXPERIMENTAL FOREST

Description: A tree plantation with more than forty species of trees planted in orderly stands. The site has the largest planted coniferous forest in North Dakota, and during migrations attracts unusual birds of the boreal forest and Rocky Mountains. Other animals to look for are white-tailed deer, wild turkeys, cottontail rabbits, ground squirrels, and tree squirrels.

Viewing Information: Of particular interest might be pine siskin and black-backed woodpeckers. White-tailed deer and turkeys can be seen in the early morning and around dusk in summer and fall. You can drive through the plantations of ponderosa pine, scotch pine, and Rocky Mountain juniper (there are many others as well), and there is a .25-mile (.5-mile round-trip) hiking trail to the top of a small hill where you can look over row upon row of trees. A gravel road provides access to this trail. Other roads through the site are sandy and may be impassable during periods of heavy snow or when it is very dry and the sand is loose.

Directions: *From Towner, go 13.5 miles west on U.S. 2. Turn south on the gravel road for one mile. Turn east for 200 yards to the hiking trail.*

Ownership: USFS (250-4443), managed by Towner State Nursery (537-5636)
Size: 636 acres   **Closest Town:** Towner

The planted evergreen forest at the Denbigh Experimental Forest attracts birds more typical of the Rocky Mountains. KEITH KRAMER

Description: A shallow, semi-permanent wetland interspersed with stands of cattails, bulrush, and other wetland plants. Upland areas have both native grasses and exotic grasses and forbs. Remnant shelterbelts and patches of shrubs contribute to making the site a mosaic of diverse habitats. Of particular interest are spectacular concentrations of snow geese in spring and fall. Giant Canada geese have been re-introduced here. In wet years, waterfowl stay on the refuge through the summer. White-tailed deer can be seen year-round.

Viewing Information: Be at the refuge at sunrise or late in the evening during spring and fall migrations. Peak months for snow geese are April to early May and again mid-September to mid-October. Giant Canada geese can be viewed in artificial nesting structures along the road in May. Ducks and broods are visible in the wetland vegetation until July. Best times for white-tailed deer are early morning and late evening throughout the summer. There is a twelve-foot observation tower overlooking Lake Alice, and two parking lots overlook Chain Lakes. Roads to the site are gravel, and can be muddy in wet weather and are occasionally blocked by snow drifts in winter. Maps of the refuge are available at the refuge entrance north of Penn.

Directions: *From Devils Lake, take U.S. 2 northwest to Penn. Turn north at Penn and go 6.5 miles to the entrance to the refuge. Pick up a map of the refuge here. Continue on the gravel road to the parking areas and the observation tower.*

Ownership: USFWS (662-8611)
Size: 12,179 acres   **Closest Town:** Penn

Redheads and canvasbacks are North Dakota's most common diving ducks. These birds will dive beneath the surface of the water to feed as opposed to dabbling ducks like mallards which tip tail-up to feed on shallow plants, seeds, and snails.

WILLIAM K. VINJE

77 GRAHAMS ISLAND STATE PARK & MINNEWAUKAN FLATS

Description: A state park and a four-mile drive through marshes, meadows, and mudflats at the western end of Devils Lake. The area attracts large numbers of migrating and nesting water birds. Among these are snow geese, Canada geese, tundra swans, western grebes, pintails, mallards, white pelicans, black-crowned night herons, great blue herons, Franklin's gulls, and double- crested cormorants. In the park there is a good viewing opportunity for white-tailed deer, turkeys, beaver, tree squirrels, ground squirrels, and birds of prey, particularly owls.

Viewing Information: The park offers viewing by car along park roads, on foot along the shoreline of Devils Lake, and by boat. Minnewaukan Flats is a four-mile drive (the land on either side of the road is private) west of the park and east of the town of Minnewaukan. The road passes through marshes and mudflats and crosses the lake. The best months for geese are April and May and September and October. Herons, gulls, cormorants, and terns nest June and July. Songbirds are in the park throughout the summer.

Directions: *From the junction of North Dakota 19 and U.S. 2 in Devils Lake, go west on North Dakota 19 approximately ten miles. Turn south for five miles, then turn east to the park. To Minnewaukan Flats, go north one mile after leaving the park, then turn west toward the town of Minnewaukan.*

Ownership: Grahams Island State Park—NDPT (766-4015); Minnewaukan Flats—PVT
Size: 1,122 acres
Closest Town: Minnewaukan

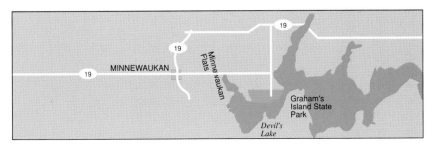

The northern shrike, sometimes called the butcher bird, is a predatory bird that impales its victims on barbed wire or thorns.

78 DEVILS LAKE LEMNA PROJECT

Description: Natural and manmade wetlands used to purify waste water from the town of Devils Lake. The site is named for lemna or duckweed, which is grown and harvested as the final water treatment. Harvested duckweed is used as fertilizer. The site is being developed as an observation area for waterfowl.

Viewing Information: Viewing is possible from your car or from three viewing mounds which, in future, will have viewing towers. The settling ponds and lemna canals are on the south side of the highway, and a large cattail marsh is on the north side. Viewing of giant Canada geese is excellent April through June. Mallards, gadwalls, shovellers, blue-winged teal, coots, and Wilson's phalaropes, are seen April-October, with wood ducks in June-July.

Directions: *From Devils Lake, go .5 mile west on North Dakota 19. The site is on both sides of the highway.*

Ownership: City of Devils Lake (662-7614)
Size: 750 acres   **Closest Town:** Devils Lake

79 SULLYS HILL NATIONAL GAME PRESERVE

Description: Rolling glacial moraine hills on the south shore of Devils Lake, featuring mature mixed hardwood forest, native grassland, and brushland. Wildlife includes re-introduced herds of bison, elk, and white-tailed deer; there are prairie dogs, fox, raccoons, skunks, weasels, mink, squirrels, muskrats, beaver, and woodchucks. The preserve's bird list of 269 species includes loons, eagles, bluebirds, and many warblers; also many water birds such as giant Canada geese, tundra swans, wood ducks, many species of dabbling ducks, herons, egrets, and marbled godwits. A separate prairie tract provides a showy wildflower display all summer.

Viewing Information: A four-mile self-guided auto tour (open early May to late October) provides viewing for the big-game enclosure, and a prairie dog town. Walking access is not permitted in the big-game enclosure because of potentially dangerous animals. Outside the enclosure are picnic areas (open May to October) and a mile-long nature trail. In winter, a 1.5-mile cross-country ski trail is maintained. The preserve is open 8 a.m. to sunset daily.

Directions: *From Devils Lake, go south on NorthDakota 57 thirteen miles, and turn south on BIA Road 6. Follow the signs to the preserve.*

Ownership: USFWS (766-4272)
Size: 1,675 acres   **Closest Town:** Fort Totten

80   LAKE WASHINGTON WILDLIFE MANAGEMENT AREA

Description: A large alkali lake surrounded by oak trees, rolling grassland, and brushland. The area features white-tailed deer, a number of nesting ducks, upland birds, wading birds, and songbirds.

Viewing Information: The probability of viewing nesting ducks and wading birds is high, especially in the northwest corner of the WMA. White-tailed deer are abundant, and there are usually substantial populations of sharp-tailed grouse, gray partridge, and pheasants. In years when frost permits, juneberries, plums, and crab apples attract a variety of songbirds. Good gravel roads around the site permit easy access, and trails wind through the area.

Directions: *From McHenry, go north eight miles on North Dakota 20 to the junction with North Dakota 15. Go west on North Dakota 15 for six miles. Take the first gravel road north (Eddy County Road 8) for approximately 4.5 miles to the entrance signs for the WMA.*

Ownership: NDGF (683-4900)
Size: 970 acres   **Closest Town:** McHenry

Related to skunks and weasels, badgers have a well-deserved reputation for toughness. They are mostly nocturnal—look for them early in the morning in open, grassy areas, especially near prairie dog towns. C. D. GRONDAHL

AUDUBON NATIONAL WILDLIFE REFUGE

Description: A reservoir surrounded by rolling native and planted grassland, cropland, and numerous small cattail marshes. The site's bird list includes 221 species, among them sandhill cranes, Canada geese, bald eagles, many species of ducks, tundra swans, black-crowned night herons, and many of the smaller sandpipers. The site has common small mammals and beaver, coyotes, foxes, and white-tailed deer.

Viewing Information: The primary developed viewing opportunity is an eight-mile auto tour that follows the shoreline of the lake through the refuge's different habitats. A brochure (available at a kiosk at the beginning of the tour) describes significant areas and habitats; the wildlife you see depends on the season. Sandhill cranes and tundra swans are abundant in fall, usually in October. Giant Canada geese usually arrive in spring and nest in elevated structures which can be seen along the tour route. By May, there are broods of goslings. The best time for bald eagles is November and December. Although the tour is designed for autos, you are encouraged to get out of your car and explore on your own. In winter, snowdrifts close the tour road.

Directions: *From Coleharbor, go two miles north on U.S. 83, then east .75 mile to viewing area.*

Ownership: USFWS (442-5474)
Size: 14,738 acres   **Closest Town:** Coleharbor

Canada geese in North Dakota have benefited greatly from artificial nesting structures placed in the state's wetlands. Geese prefer sites that have good visibility, access to water, and are safe from predators.
MIKE BEILKE

93

POPULAR WILDLIFE VIEWING SPECIES
IN NORTH DAKOTA—AND WHERE TO FIND THEM

The list below features some of the more interesting, uncommon, or attractive wildlife found in North Dakota. It is a sampling of species and not meant to be an inclusive list.

SPECIES	SITE NUMBER
American Avocet	8, 10, 37, 64, 65
American Bittern	10, 23, 34, 46, 69
Audubon's Warbler	53
Baird's Sparrow	32, 64, 65, 67, 74
Bald Eagle	27, 40, 41, 42, 59, 61
Beaver	2, 7, 17, 19, 40, 81
Bighorn Sheep	54, 55
Bison	25, 43, 56, 60, 79
Black-crowned Night Heron	10, 20, 74, 77
Bobolink	16
Brewer's Sparrow	51
Canada Geese	27, 28, 46, 62, 65
Canvasback Ducks	27, 30, 62
Chestnut-collared Longspur	51
Clark's Nutcracker	52
Coyote	34, 59, 74, 81
Elk	56, 58, 72, 79
Fox	12, 19, 23, 79, 81
Golden Eagle	51, 54, 55, 56, 59, 60
Gray (Hungarian) Partridge	21, 28, 29, 57, 80
Great Blue Heron	10, 46, 49, 77, 79
LeConte's Sparrow	66, 67, 74
Marbled Godwit	8, 64, 79
Mink	12, 19, 71, 72, 79
Moose	1, 3, 17, 68, 72
Mule Deer	52, 53, 55, 56, 59, 60
Muskrat	61, 69, 71, 72, 79
Paddlefish	61
Painted Turtles	9, 69
Pileated Woodpecker	4
Pinnated Grouse (Prairie Chicken)	18
Piping Plover	32, 44, 57

SPECIES	SITE NUMBER

North Dakota's most common ground squirrel, the thirteen-lined ground squirrel is found throughout the state. Active during daylight, they are most commonly seen along roadsides. KEITH KRAMER

About Defenders of Wildlife

For more than four decades, Defenders of Wildlife has been one of America's most effective champions of wildlife. With wildlife populations declining at accelerating rates, Defenders is promoting new approaches to wildlife conservation that will help species get ahead of the extinction curve. A nonprofit origination founded in 1947, Defenders has over 80,000 members and supporters. Defenders utilizes public education, litigation, and advocacy of progressive public policies aimed at protecting the diversity of wildlife and preserving the habitat critical to its survival.

If you are interested in becoming a member, annual dues are $20, which includes six issues of the bimonthly magazine, *Defenders*. For further information, write or call:

Defenders of Wildlife
1244 19th St. N.W.
Washington, DC 20036
(202) 659-9510

More Books From Falcon Press

The *North Dakota Wildlife Viewing Guide* is part of the Watchable Wildlife Series from Falcon Press. This series has been created through the National Wildlife Viewing Program, a Watchable Wildlife partnership initiative coordinated by Defenders of Wildlife. If you liked this book, look for the companion guides that cover other states you plan to visit.

In addition to the Watchable Wildlife Series, Falcon Press specializes in full-color nature books, calendars, and recreational guidebooks. If you want to know more about hiking, fishing, scenic driving, river floating, or rockhounding in your favorite state, check with your local bookstore or call toll-free 1-800-582-2665. When you call, please ask for a free catalog listing all the books and calendars available from Falcon Press.

Falcon Press Publishing Co., Inc.
P.O. Box 1718
Helena, MT 59624
1-800-582-2665